THE SCOTTISH PARLIAMENT

AN INTRODUCTION

THE SCOTTISH PARLIAMENT

◆

AN INTRODUCTION

Jean McFadden

Senior Lecturer in Law, University of Strathclyde

Mark Lazarowicz

Advocate

T&T CLARK
EDINBURGH
2000

T&T CLARK LTD
59 GEORGE STREET
EDINBURGH EH2 2LQ
SCOTLAND

First published 1999
Second Edition 2000

ISBN 0 567 00560 7

British Library Cataloguing-in-Publication Data
A catalogue record for this book is available from the British Library

Typeset by Fakenham Photosetting Limited, Fakenham, Norfolk
Printed and bound in Scotland by Bell & Bain Ltd, Glasgow

PREFACE

It used to be said that what distinguished the British political system from practically every other country in the world was the absence of a written constitution. The extent to which that statement is true has become significantly smaller in the last 25 years, as a result of the UK joining the European Community and becoming bound by the Treaty of Rome and its successors. Now the combined effect of the Human Rights Act and the Scotland Act, when added to the European treaties, means that in Scotland the rights of individuals and the powers of the state are, to a considerable extent, based on fundamental constitutional laws which together can truly be said to be the written constitution of Scotland.

This book aims to be a concise, but comprehensive, guide to that part of the Scottish constitution which is based on the Scotland Act 1998. It seeks to place the constitutional settlement which that Act represents in its historical setting, as well as the internal context of the Scottish Parliament's relations with local government, and the external context of its relations with the Westminster Parliament and Europe. It also looks at the likely procedures and internal working arrangements of the Parliament, based on the recommendations of the Consultative Steering Group which provided all-party advice to the Government on these matters. (At the time of writing, the Statutory Instruments which are expected to put these recommendations into effect had not yet been published.)

The authors wish to thank William Bain, Arnold Bell, Kenneth Campbell, and Patricia Hogg for helpful comments on the text. They would also like to thank Alan Barr, Lynda Clark, Q.C., M.P., and Neil Davidson, Q.C. for advice on some particular issues considered in the book. They are also indebted to Patricia Hogg and Mhairi Paterson for preparing the index. Thanks are also due to the staff of the Scottish Parliament for helpful advice on a number of factual matters concerning the operation of the Parliament. Jean McFadden expresses her thanks to Dale McFadzean for teaching her time-saving tricks on the computer and for work on Tables 2A–2C. Thanks also to Andrew Mylne, Clerk of Public Bills in the Scottish Parliament, for helpful comments on Tables 2A–2C. The Tables are based on the Table in Guidance on Public Bills published by the Stationery Office (1st edn, 1999). The authors, of course, accept full responsibility for any errors and omissions.

The authors acknowledge the permission given by Her Majesty's Stationery Office to reproduce the map on page 105.

Jean McFadden
Mark Lazarowicz
April 2000

CONTENTS

1. THE SCOTTISH PARLIAMENT: THE BACKGROUND

INTRODUCTION

The Scotland Act 1998[1] is one of the most important constitutional statutes passed by the UK Parliament for a very long time. It is of significance both for Scotland and for the rest of the UK. In Scottish terms, it establishes a parliament which has the powers to make laws for Scotland in a wide range of areas. In UK terms, it is part of a package of devolutionary or decentralising measures which include a National Assembly for Wales, with mainly administrative powers, and an Assembly in Northern Ireland, with legislative powers. The establishment of these institutions represents a significant transfer of power from the UK Parliament and may in time lead to the establishment of regional assemblies in England.

SCOTLAND AND THE UNION[2]

Prior to 1707, England and Scotland possessed separate constitutions and parliaments. Scotland and England came together in a political union in 1707 after the Parliaments of England and Scotland passed individual Acts of Union whereby the separate Parliaments of the two countries ceased to exist and were replaced by the Parliament of the United Kingdom of Great Britain. Although the Scottish Parliament was abolished in 1707, the Scots maintained a sense of national identity due, in part, to the fact that the Presbyterian Church and the Scottish legal system were preserved by the terms of the Union. The union was not warmly embraced by most Scots. Indeed, there was rioting on the streets of Glasgow and Edinburgh when the terms were first made public. However, the economic situation at the time was such that acceptance of the union was almost inevitable and it was largely tolerated. The arrangements for the government of Scotland from London were, for much of the eighteenth and nineteenth centuries, in the hands of the Lord Advocate, a Law Officer appointed by the government. Interest in Parliamentary affairs by Scots was minimal as their MPs were manipulated to dance to the government's tune. The electoral system was so corrupt and the number of people entitled to vote so tiny that not even the Scottish

---

[1] All references in this book to sections and Schedules which do not specify the legislation concerned are references to the Scotland Act 1998, unless it is clear from the context that other legislation is being referred to.

[2] For further reading on the political and historical background, see the books by Alice Brown *et al.*, Michael Fry, and James Kellas, in the list of "Further Reading" at the end of this book.

aristocracy, let alone the ordinary Scot, could hope to achieve influence. In 1823 it was estimated that fewer than 3000 men were entitled to vote. (Women were not to get the vote until 1918). However, demand for electoral reform grew and, in 1832, the male middle classes were enfranchised by the Representation of the People (Scotland) Act, followed by the Representation of the People Acts of 1867 and 1884 which extended the franchise to include all men aged 21 years or over. As more and more men were given the vote, discontent rose about the lack of interest shown by the Westminster Parliament in Scottish affairs.

THE ROAD TO DEVOLUTION

Demand grew for the appointment of a Scottish Secretary of State, a post which had been abolished in 1746. In 1885, the government passed the Secretary for Scotland Act which established the post of Secretary for Scotland and the Scottish Office, based in Dover House in London. In 1926, the post was upgraded to that of Secretary of State and in 1939 the Scottish Office was moved to St. Andrew's House in Edinburgh. The Secretary of State for Scotland has had a seat in the Cabinet in peacetime since 1892.

A number of factors, including the rise of the Irish Home Rule movement in the nineteenth century led to the emergence of a Scottish Home Rule Association in 1886. Scottish home rule was frequently discussed in the House of Commons although no bill reached the statute book to provide a parliament for Scotland, similar to that which was provided for Northern Ireland by the Government of Ireland Act 1920.

The National Party for Scotland was founded in 1928 and started to contest elections in the following year. In 1934, the National Party of Scotland merged with another home rule party, the Scottish Party, to form the Scottish National Party (SNP). The SNP won its first parliamentary seat in a by-election in Motherwell in 1945 but lost it in the general election later that year. The SNP made no more headway in terms of parliamentary seats for over 20 years but gained an increasing number of votes, particularly in by-elections. In 1967, they won the previously safe Labour seat of Hamilton in a by-election and in the following year they won 30 per cent of the vote and 108 seats in the local government elections.

The Labour Government, concerned by the electoral success of the SNP and of the Welsh nationalist party, Plaid Cymru, which had won a Welsh by-election in 1966, appointed, in 1969, a Royal Commission (chaired by Lord Crowther and after his death by Lord Kilbrandon) to examine the constitution of the UK. The Commission reported in 1973.[3] It rejected separatism and federalism as solutions and recommended a directly elected assembly for Scotland, elected on the system of the single transferable vote. The response to the

---

[3]Cmnd. 5460.

Commission's report by the Conservative and Labour parties was lukewarm and neither party included devolution in their manifestos for the general election which was held in February 1974. The results of that election, however, gave devolution a new lease of life as the SNP won seven seats and Plaid Cymru two seats.

The new Labour Government, which did not have an outright majority of seats in the House of Commons, was forced to make concessions to the nationalist parties and announced that it would bring forward proposals for consideration. In September 1974, a White Paper was published entitled *Democracy and Devolution: proposals for Scotland and Wales.*[4] It proposed directly elected assemblies for Scotland and Wales, with the Scottish Assembly having legislative, but not tax-raising, powers and the Welsh Assembly having executive powers only. A further general election was held in October 1974 at which the SNP won 11 seats. A second White Paper was published in November 1975 entitled *Our Changing Democracy: Devolution to Scotland and Wales.*[5] A Scotland and Wales Bill was published in November 1976 but the Government, lacking a secure majority, was unable to get it through all the necessary stages in Parliament and the Bill was dropped. The following year, separate Bills for Scotland and Wales were introduced. During the Parliamentary process an amendment was introduced which made it necessary for 40 per cent of the electorates to vote "Yes" in referenda before the Acts could be brought into operation. The Scotland and the Wales Acts received the Royal Assent in 1978 and the referenda were held in March 1979. Although the majority of Scots who did vote voted "Yes", the 40 per cent threshold was not reached. The Welsh decisively voted "No". A motion of no confidence in the Labour Government was tabled, the Government was defeated and a general election was held in May 1979 which was won by the Conservatives under Margaret Thatcher. The Scotland and the Wales Acts were repealed in the following month.

THE SCOTTISH CONSTITUTIONAL CONVENTION

The Conservative Government remained in power for 18 years and was implacably opposed to devolution but the desire for some form of devolution in Scotland remained and a cross-party Campaign for a Scottish Assembly (CSA) was formed in 1980. Following the re-election of the Conservatives in 1983 and 1987, the CSA set up a committee of prominent Scots who produced *The Claim of Right for Scotland* in 1988 which advocated the establishment of a constitutional convention to draw up plans for Scottish self-government. The Scottish Constitutional Convention (SCC) was set up in March 1989 with the involvement of the Labour and Liberal parties and several smaller parties, but without the Conservatives and the SNP. Also in

---

[4]Cmnd. 5732.
[5]Cmnd. 6348.

membership were most of the Scottish local authorities and representatives of a wide spectrum of Scottish life. The SCC published a
number of documents culminating in *Scotland's Parliament: Scotland's
Right* (November 1995) which advocated a Scottish Parliament elected
partly by the traditional "first past the post" system and partly by a
form of proportional representation. The SCC recommended that the
Parliament should have legislative powers over a wide range of
domestic issues and the power to vary income tax by up to three
pence in the pound.

THE 1997 GENERAL ELECTION AND THE REFERENDUM

The Labour Party and the Liberal Democrat Party included a commitment to a Scottish Parliament, based on the proposals of the SCC, in
their manifestos for the 1997 General Election. The Labour Party won
that election with a very large majority and within three months
published a White Paper, *Scotland's Parliament*,[6] which detailed their
plans for a devolved parliament with legislative and limited tax-
varying powers. Before introducing a Bill to establish the parliament,
the Government wanted the proposal to be endorsed by the Scottish
people in a referendum. The Referendums Act 1997 was quickly
passed by the UK Parliament and a referendum was held in
September 1997. The electorate had to vote on two issues — on the
principle of a Scottish Parliament, and on its tax-varying powers. The
answers which the Scottish people gave to both questions was
emphatically in the affirmative. On the issue of a Scottish Parliament,
74.3 per cent of those who did vote voted "Yes" (a total of 1,775,045
voters). On the issue of tax-varying powers, 63.5 per cent voted "Yes"
(1,512,889 voters).

The government introduced the Scotland Bill into the House of
Commons in December 1997. The Bill received the Royal Assent on
19th November 1998. The first general election to the Scottish Parliament was held on 6th May 1999. The Parliament was formally opened
by the Queen on 1st July 1999 and on that date the Parliament
assumed its full powers. The following chapters deal with various
aspects of the Scottish Parliament, including elections, the powers of
the Parliament, and how it goes about its business. The Scottish
Government and the powers of the First Minister and other Ministers
are examined as are relations with the UK Parliament and how legal
disputes will be resolved. The vital area of financing the Parliament is
also examined. Finally, there is discussion of the relationships
between the Parliament and local government and the Parliament and
Europe.

---

[6]Cm. 3658.

2. THE POWERS OF THE PARLIAMENT

INTRODUCTION

The form of government which the establishment of a Scottish Parliament brings to Scotland is known as legislative devolution. This means that the UK Parliament has voluntarily transferred a number of its law-making powers to the Scottish Parliament without relinquishing its own supreme authority or sovereignty. The Scottish Parliament is not independent. It is not free to make laws in any area which it chooses. Therefore, there has to be a framework which defines the areas in which it has the power to make laws (its legislative competence) and those areas where the UK Parliament has not relinquished its law-making power. We must, then, examine how the UK Parliament has gone about setting that framework. We must also consider the impact of the legal doctrine known as the sovereignty of Parliament.

THE DIVISION OF POWERS – TWO BASIC MODELS

In any system of government where powers are divided between two levels, central and regional, state or provincial, the possibility of one level of government trespassing into the legislative or executive territory of the other may arise. Therefore, the powers of each must be set out in a written document. In the vast majority of countries this document will be the constitution. However, since the UK does not have a constitution contained in one single document the powers of the two levels of government are set out in an Act of Parliament. In the case of Scotland, the Act of Parliament is the Scotland Act 1998.

Broadly speaking, there are two basic models for the constitution or the Act of Parliament to follow:

- the central authority devolves all of its powers to the local or subordinate body except for certain powers which it specifically reserves to itself;
- the central authority devolves to the local or subordinate body certain specified powers while everything not so specified is, by implication, reserved to the centre.

The former is called the retaining model, and the latter the transferring model. Put simply, the retaining model spells out what the subordinate or local body *cannot* do and it is implied that it *can* do everything not spelled out. The transferring model spells out what the local or subordinate body *can* do and it is implied that it *cannot* do anything which is not mentioned.

The American Constitution is an example of the retaining model. The powers of the United States Congress (the federal or central legislature) are set out in Article 1. The powers of the states, known as "residuary" powers are set out in the Tenth Amendment to the Constitution as follows: "The powers not delegated to the United States by the Constitution, nor prohibited by it to the States, are reserved to the States respectively or to the people". The American model thus tilts the balance, at least in theory, against the centre, as everything not specified in the Constitution lies within the powers of the individual states.

The Canadian Constitution is an example of the transferring model and was designed to produce a strong central government. Section 91 of the British North America Act 1867, now known as the Constitution Act 1867, allocates national powers to the central or federal Parliament, while section 92 allocates regional powers to the provincial legislatures. Section 91, however, also gives the federal Parliament the power "to make laws for the peace, order and good government of Canada in relation to all matters not coming within the classes of subjects assigned exclusively to the Provinces ...".

The Scotland Act 1978 which was to have established a Scottish Assembly in 1979 was an example of the transferring model, specifying in great detail the legislative and executive powers which were to be devolved from Westminster. Schedule 10 to the Act listed 25 groups of matters which were to be devolved matters and another 25 which were specifically not included in those groups. There then followed a lengthy list of Acts of Parliament, going back to the Anatomy Act of 1832, and an indication of the extent to which each Act was or was not included in the groups of devolved matters. Schedule 11 then listed the matters which were within the powers of the Scottish Executive but not within the law-making powers of the Scottish Assembly. Schedule 16 contained another lengthy list, this time of amendments of Acts of the UK Parliament. The Act was extremely complex, would have required frequent updating to take account of new and amended legislation, and would have led to many challenges in court as to whether the Assembly was acting outwith its powers (*ultra vires*).

Three pieces of legislation for Northern Ireland give examples of the retaining model, the Government of Ireland Act 1920, the Northern Ireland Constitution Act 1973, and the Northern Ireland Act 1998.

The Government of Ireland Act 1920 which established the Northern Ireland Parliament at Stormont listed, not the devolved powers, but the powers reserved to Westminster. Section 4 of the Act provides that:

"Subject to the provisions of this Act ... the Parliament of Northern Ireland shall ... have powers to make laws for the peace, order and good government of Northern Ireland with the following limitations ... that they shall not have powers to make laws in respect of the following matters in particular, namely ..."

There follows a list of 14 areas reserved to Westminster including, among others, the Crown, the making of peace or war, and the armed forces.

The Northern Ireland Constitution Act 1973 established the short-lived Northern Ireland Assembly and the power-sharing executive (it lasted for the first five months of 1974). Section 4(1) of the Act states: "Laws may be made for Northern Ireland by Measures of the Assembly". Matters excepted from the law-making powers of the Assembly were listed in Schedule 2 to the Act and included, among others, the Crown, the armed forces, and international relations.

The Northern Ireland Act 1998 established the Northern Ireland Assembly following the Belfast "Good Friday" agreement earlier that year. Once again, this gave the assembly the power to make laws in all areas which were not specifically excluded from its competence. Schedule 2 to the Act lists "excepted matters" which are permanently outside the competence of the Assembly, and Schedule 3 to the Act lists "reserved matters", over which the Assembly may legislate, but only with the consent of the Secretary of State for Northern Ireland. Section 4(2) of the Act also gives the Secretary of State the power to remove matters from the list of reserved matters so that the Assembly then has the power to legislate in such areas without his or her consent (and also to put matters concerning which legislation did not previously need his consent *onto* the list of reserved matters).

THE SCOTLAND ACT 1998

The Scottish Constitutional Convention, early on in its life, adopted the principle of the sovereignty of the Scottish people, which led it to favour the retaining form of constitution. In its first report, *Towards a Scottish Parliament*, it declared that "The type of statute which sits most easily with that principle is the retaining one; it reflects a constitutional settlement in which the Scottish people, being sovereign, agree to the exercise of specified powers by Westminster but retain their sovereignty over all other matters."[1] In its later reports, the issue was not explicitly addressed but it appears that the Scottish Constitutional Convention expected that any new Scotland Act would, like the 1978 Act, list the powers and responsibilities to be devolved from Westminster on the grounds that the UK Parliament would be unwilling to adopt the form of the Government of Ireland Act in the mistaken belief that it might be giving away too much power.

The Constitution Unit examined the two forms and, in its report

---

[1]*Towards a Scottish Parliament* (Scottish Constitutional Convention, 1989) p 36.

Scotland's Parliament: Fundamentals for a New Scotland Act,[2] recommended strongly that the best method of ensuring legal clarity as to the scope of devolution was to specify the powers to be retained by Westminster and devolve the remainder. It rejected the view that this was, of necessity, a more generous approach. The method is neutral. It is the length and complexity of the list of retained powers which determines the level of generosity.

The Scottish Office had the benefit of the work of both the Scottish Constitutional Convention and the Constitution Unit in drawing up the White Paper, *Scotland's Parliament,* and the Scotland Bill. Specific reference is made in the White Paper to the Northern Ireland model and the Government opted for the retaining model in the Scotland Bill. All matters which are not specifically reserved to the UK Parliament are devolved to the Scottish Parliament. From all accounts, the Secretary of State for Scotland seems to have played his hand particularly skilfully in the Cabinet to ensure that this was the form of legislation adopted.

THE SCOTTISH PARLIAMENT AND THE SOVEREIGNTY OF THE UK PARLIAMENT

As far as law-making powers are concerned, the important parts of the Scotland Act are sections 28–30 and Schedule 5, which lists the powers which are retained by, or reserved to, the UK Parliament. Schedule 4, which sets out various enactments protected from modification by the Scottish Parliament, is also significant. Before we examine these, however, mention should be made of the UK constitutional doctrine of the sovereignty of parliament. The sovereignty of the UK Parliament is perhaps the most important doctrine of constitutional law in the UK. In its absolute form it means that the UK Parliament is the one supreme law-making body in the UK and can, in theory, pass any law that it wishes. Its laws cannot be declared invalid even by the highest court in the land, the House of Lords. This is not the case in federal states such as the United States or Germany where there is a written constitution and a supreme court which can strike down a law as invalid if it is in conflict with the constitution. The sovereignty of the UK Parliament has undoubtedly been modified by our membership of the European Communities but as far as domestic or national law is concerned, the doctrine remains firmly in place. Thus, any parliament or assembly created by the UK Parliament is a subordinate body. It is not independent nor is it co-ordinate with central government as in a federal system. It may not only be overruled by the UK Parliament, it may even be abolished by it. Of course, this is legal theory and account has to be taken of practical politics. If the Scottish Parliament is a popular institution, no

---

[2]*Scotland's Parliament: Fundamentals for a New Scotland Act* (London, 1996). The Constitution Unit is a research project, based in University College, London. It has published a number of reports dealing with issues of constitutional reform.

government at Westminster would want to incur the wrath of the Scottish electorate by interfering with the Scottish Parliament without good cause.

THE LAW-MAKING POWERS OF THE PARLIAMENT

Bearing this in mind, let us examine the law-making powers of the Scottish Parliament. The powers are contained in sections 28–30. Section 28 states that, subject to various exceptions in section 29, the Scottish Parliament has the power to make laws which will be known as Acts of the Scottish Parliament. Proposed Acts are to be known as Bills, as at Westminster, and once Bills have passed through the Parliamentary stages and received the Royal Assent they become Acts. However, the final subsection of section 28 states that the power of the Parliament of the UK to make laws for Scotland remains unaffected. This is an assertion of the sovereignty of the UK Parliament. The UK Parliament can, by passing an Act at Westminster, override or nullify any Act of the Scottish Parliament and if the Scottish Parliament refuses to pass an Act which the Government at Westminster wishes it to pass, the UK Parliament will simply pass one for it. However, if there are good working relationships between the two Parliaments and goodwill on both sides, it is unlikely that the UK Parliament will wish to assert its sovereignty in this way. As it is in the retaining form, the Scotland Act does not list the areas in which the Scottish Parliament has the power to legislate. Instead, it lists the areas in which it cannot legislate, some of which are found in section 29 and the remainder in Schedules 4 and 5.

Section 29 sets out a number of areas where any attempt by the Scottish Parliament to make law would be invalid:

- it cannot pass a valid law any provision of which would form part of the law of any country or territory other than Scotland or confer or remove functions which are exercisable except in or as regards Scotland. While it is extremely unlikely that the Scottish Parliament would want to pass a law for, say, France or Indonesia, this is designed to prevent it legislating, presumably inadvertently, for any other part of the UK;
- it cannot pass a valid law any provision of which is incompatible with those parts of the European Convention on Human Rights which are to be given effect by the Human Rights Act 1998;
- it cannot pass a valid law any provision of which is incompatible with European Community law. Although relations with the European Community are reserved to the UK Parliament, the Scottish Parliament is responsible for observing and implementing the various obligations under Community law in relation to devolved matters;
- it cannot pass a valid law any provision of which would remove the Lord Advocate from his position as head of the systems of criminal prosecution and investigation of deaths in

Scotland. This is one of various measures in the Scotland Act designed to protect the independence of the Scottish Law officers;

- it cannot pass a valid law any provision of which relates to matters which are reserved to the UK Parliament. These provisions are listed in Schedule 5 and are dealt with below;
- it cannot pass a valid law any provision of which modifies any of the enactments listed in Schedule 4. These are also dealt with below.

Section 30 enables Schedules 4 and 5 to be modified at a later stage by a parliamentary order known as an Order in Council. This enables the UK Parliament to make changes to the contents of these schedules without the necessity of passing another Act of Parliament.

RESERVED MATTERS

The matters reserved to the UK Parliament are areas into which the Scottish Parliament may not trespass. Any attempt to make law in any of these areas would be invalid. The Scottish Constitutional Convention recommended that the primary matters which should be retained by the UK Parliament should be defence, foreign affairs, immigration, nationality, social security policy, and central economic and fiscal responsibilities. The White Paper, *Scotland's Parliament*, added to the list the constitution of the UK, common markets for UK goods and services, employment legislation, the regulation of certain professions, transport safety and regulation and a miscellany of other matters including the regulatory framework for broadcasting, abortion, and equality legislation. The general justification is that there are many matters which can be more effectively and beneficially handled on a UK basis.[3]

When translated into the Scotland Act the reserved matters are set out in considerable detail (18 pages) in Schedule 5. The Schedule is divided into three parts, Part I dealing with what are called General Reservations, Part II dealing with Specific Reservations and Part III dealing with various miscellaneous matters under General Provisions.

General Reservations Part I

1. Various aspects of the constitution of the UK are reserved. These are:

- the Crown, including succession to the Crown and a regency;
- the Union of the Kingdoms of Scotland and England;
- the Parliament of the United Kingdom;
- the continued existence of the High Court of Justiciary and the Court of Session.

Thus, it will not be open to the Scottish Parliament to restore the

---

[3]Para 3.2.

Stuarts to the throne and the eighteenth century Acts relating to the Hanoverian Protestant succession will continue to apply to the succession to the throne on the death or abdication of the present Queen unless the UK Parliament deems otherwise.[4] Nor will it be possible for the Scottish Parliament to declare Scotland independent even if a majority of MSPs are members of the Scottish National Party, as that would affect, among other things, the union of the kingdoms which took place in 1603. The continued existence of the Scottish Courts was guaranteed in the Acts of Union of 1707 and that is further confirmed by this reservation.

2. The aspects of foreign affairs which are reserved include:

- international relations with territories outside the UK, the European Communities and other international organisations;
- the regulation of international trade;
- international development assistance.

The *observation and implementation* of various international obligations including the Human Rights Convention and obligations under EC law are not reserved. The Scottish Parliament is able, therefore, and in fact may be required, to legislate for the purpose of giving effect to international obligations as far as they relate to devolved matters. In the case of EC obligations, the Scottish Ministers may be liable under EC law to the same penalties as UK Ministers. Assisting UK Ministers is not reserved, and so Scottish Ministers are able to assist UK Ministers in the formulation, negotiation and implementation of policy relating to international obligations and are able to participate in European Council meetings and in meetings with our partners in the European Union.

3. The reservations relating to defence include:

- the defence of the realm;
- the army, navy and air forces and reserve forces;
- visiting forces international headquarters and defence organisations;
- trading with the enemy and enemy property.

Thus, all the matters for which the Ministry of Defence is responsible are covered by these reservations. Civil defence, however, is not reserved: in particular, planning and organisation by civilian authorities, and the provision of non-combative defence against hostile attacks. There is also a specific exemption relating to sea fishing. The Royal Navy carries out various enforcement duties on behalf of the Fisheries Department and Scottish Ministers are able to confer powers on members of the armed forces to enable this to continue.

The other matters included in the general reservations in Part I are:

- the registration and funding of political parties;

---

[4]This did not prevent the Parliament discussing the question of the Protestant succession in December 1999, on a motion from the SNP group in the Parliament.

- the civil service;
- treason.

Specific Reservations Part II

Part II sets out specific, subject-related reservations by sections grouped under 11 heads. The heads are:

• Head A — Financial and Economic Matters

These include the issue and circulation of money, taxes and excise duties, government borrowing and lending, the exchange rate, the Bank of England and control over UK public expenditure. Specifically excepted are local taxes which partially fund local government expenditure, currently the council tax and non-domestic rates. The reservation of public expenditure does not affect the Scottish Parliament's ability to allocate its own resources. This section also reserves the currency, financial services (except fixing the dates of bank holidays), financial markets and money laundering.

• Head B — Home Affairs

This Head covers a miscellany of matters dealt with by the Home Office including various aspects of the misuse of drugs: possession, production, supply, import and export, and trafficking. The Scottish Parliament, however, has powers in key areas such as education, health, social work, and criminal prosecution. Immigration, nationality, and extradition are reserved although certain executive powers of the Secretary of State are transferred to the Scottish Ministers. National security, official secrets, the interception of communication, and terrorism are reserved under this head as are firearms, data protection, and scientific procedures on live animals. Elections to the House of Commons, the European Parliament and the Scottish Parliament itself are reserved but the Scottish Parliament has power to legislate for all aspects of local government elections except for the franchise. (The Parliament could, therefore, change the electoral system for local council elections, *e.g.* by the introduction of a form of proportional representation and, indeed, one of the first acts of the Scottish Executive after the May 1999 elections was to set up a working group with a remit, amongst other things, to advise on how a such a system could be introduced).[5] Betting, gaming, lotteries, and various aspects of the classification of films and the distribution of video recordings are also reserved.

• Head C — Trade and Industry

This Head covers a large number of areas including the creation, operation, regulation, and dissolution of business associations. The phrase "business associations" covers companies, partnerships, building societies, and various other bodies. The intention of the

---

[5]The *Renewing Local Democracy Group*, chaired by Richard Kerley.

reservation is to ensure a level playing field for business within the UK. Charities and certain public bodies are excepted from this reservation. The reasoning behind the latter exception is to enable the Scottish Parliament to create and regulate public bodies which are business associations for devolved areas such as health, education, sport, urban regeneration, and the environment — areas in which Scottish quangos such as the Scottish Sports Council already exist.

Import and export control are reserved to ensure a level playing field for UK business, but as agriculture, fisheries and food are devolved the movement of food, animal, animal products, plants, animal feed, fertilisers, and pesticides is excepted from this reservation.

Insolvency, competition (except for certain practices in the Scottish legal profession), intellectual property, consumer protection (except in relation to food safety), product standards, safety, and liability (except in relation to agriculture fisheries and food) are all reserved under this Head. The regulation of sea fishing outside the Scottish zone except in relation to Scottish fishing boats is reserved as are weights and measures, telecommunications and postal services.

• Head D — Energy

The generation, distribution and supply of electricity is reserved. Most aspects of oil and gas are reserved, including the ownership of, exploration for, and exploitation of, deposits of oil and natural gas. However, the manufacture of gas is not reserved nor are the powers to provide assistance for onshore activities in support of offshore activities. Coal, including its ownership and exploitation, deep and open cast coal mining and subsidence are all reserved. The only exceptions to this reservation are certain environmental duties. Nuclear energy and installations, including nuclear safety and liability for nuclear occurrences are all reserved. However, duties in relation to the keeping and use of radioactive material, the disposal or accumulation of radioactive waste and the regulation of non-nuclear activities at nuclear installations are excepted from reservation. Energy conservation is reserved but the Scottish Parliament is specifically allowed to legislate for, and in general promote, energy efficiency.

• Head E — Transport

In the case of road transport, various aspects of road traffic regulation and road safety are reserved including the licensing of drivers, driving instruction and the licensing and registration of vehicles. The prosecution and punishment of offenders for a range of road traffic offences is also reserved. However, the Scottish Parliament will be able to legislate about the promotion of road safety by local authorities. Scottish Ministers and UK Government Ministers are given concurrent powers in relation to road safety information and training.

The provision and regulation of railway services and rail transport security are reserved as is (not surprisingly) the Channel Tunnel but the making of certain grants relating to railway services is excepted from reservation.

In the case of transport by sea, marine safety, navigation rights, the regulation of the British merchant fleet and all matters relating to the employment of seafarers are reserved. The Scottish Parliament, however, has the power to pass legislation relating to ports, harbours and piers. It also has the power to deal with the regulation of works which may endanger or obstruct navigation. An important exception from reservation is financial assistance to bulk freight shipping services between the Highlands and Islands and locations outside Scotland which are necessary for the social and economic well-being of these remote communities.

The regulation of aviation and air transport, including air safety and security are reserved as are arrangements to compensate and repatriate passengers when an air transport operator becomes insolvent. Exceptions from reservation relate mainly to the provision of airports and various airport controls.

Miscellaneous reservations under this Head cover the transport of radioactive material, standards for public passenger transport for the disabled and the carriage of dangerous goods.

• Head F — Social Security

This Head reserves social security schemes financed by central or local expenditure which provide benefits to individuals. Examples include National Insurance, the Social Fund, housing, and council tax benefits. Exceptions to this reservation include the provision in exceptional circumstances for payments to people in need and services such as home-help and residential nursing accommodation. Various provisions for the maintenance of children are also excepted although the subject matter of the Child Support Acts in general is reserved. Occupational, personal and war pensions are all reserved but the Scotland Act contains specific provision for the payment of pensions to former members and staff of the Scottish Parliament.

• Head G — Regulation of the Professions

The professions reserved are architects, the health professions, and auditors. The health professions include doctors, dentists, opticians, pharmacists, nurses, midwives and many others including veterinary surgeons. The Scottish Parliament, however, has the power to legislate on the vocational training of doctors and dentists.

• Head H — Employment

Employment rights and duties and industrial relations are reserved. The exception to this is the setting of wages for Scottish agricultural workers which comes under the remit of the Scottish Agricultural Wages Board. This means that all other matters relating to wages are not within the legislative competence of the Scottish Parliament.

Thus, the Parliament cannot legislate for a Scottish minimum wage. Health and safety at work are reserved but public safety in devolved areas is not, thus allowing the Scottish Parliament to legislate on, for example, the safety of sports grounds. Job search and support are reserved but the duties which Scottish Enterprise and Highlands and Islands Enterprise have to assist people seeking work to obtain training are excepted. Careers services are also excepted.

(there is no Head I)

• Head J — Health and Medicine

Abortion, xenotransplantation, embryology, surrogacy, and genetics are all reserved. The justification is that all of these raise major ethical issues and/or require expertise to be pooled at a UK level to allow them to be regulated satisfactorily. The Scottish Parliament will, however, be able to legislate on all other matters of sexual health. Medicines, medical supplies, and poisons are reserved as is the regulation of prices for medical supplies for the National Health Service in Scotland. Schemes for the distribution of welfare foods (milk and vitamins) are reserved.

• Head K – Media and Culture

All regulatory responsibilities relating to television and radio broad-casting are reserved although some executive functions relating to the funding of Gaelic broadcasting are transferred to the Scottish Executive. The justification for the reservation is that the regulatory framework is an important aspect of the single market in the UK and that the management of the airwaves and of competition in the in-dependent television sector requires to be carried out on a UK basis.

The Public Lending Right Scheme which provides payments to authors whose books are borrowed from public libraries is reserved as is the scheme by which the Government indemnifies lenders for the loss of or damage to works of art and other objects.

• Head L — Miscellaneous

The determination of the salaries of judges of the Court of Session, sheriffs, members of the Scottish Lands Tribunal, and the Chairman of the Scottish Land Court are reserved but payment of the salaries is not. Payment will be made out of the Scottish Consolidated Fund and will not require the prior approval of the Scottish Parliament. This is in line with UK practice and is one of the measures designed to protect the independence of the judiciary.

Most aspects of equal opportunity are reserved. Equal opportunity is defined as the prevention, elimination or regulation of discrimina-tion between persons on the grounds of sex or marital status, on racial grounds, or on grounds of disability, age, sexual orientation, language or social origin, or of other personal attributes, including beliefs or opinions, such as religious beliefs or political opinions. Excepted from reservation is the encouragement of equal opportunity and the observance of equal opportunity requirements and the imposition of duties on Scottish public bodies and cross-border public authorities with a view to securing that their functions are carried out with due regard to the need to meet equal opportunity requirements.

Also under this Head comes the control of nuclear, biological, chemical and any other weapons of mass destruction.

Timescales, time zones, and the determination of summer time are reserved along with the date of Easter and the calendar generally. Excepted are the dates of bank, public and local holidays.

The Ordnance Survey is reserved as is the regulation of activities in outer space.

General Provisions Part III

This part of Schedule 5 safeguards from reservation Scottish public bodies with no reserved functions and those which have mixed functions, some reserved and some devolved. It also safeguards the giving of financial assistance to industry to promote or sustain economic development or employment. This part also reserves the constitution, assets, liabilities, funding, and receipts of all the bodies reserved by name in Part II and specifically the Commission for Racial Equality, the Equal Opportunities Commission and the National Disability Council.

Thus it can be seen that, although the UK Government decided to use the retaining model for the division of responsibilities between the Scottish and the UK Parliaments, the list of reserved powers is very detailed. The list may be modified from time to time by an Order in Council. The Scottish Parliament is, however, free to make laws in all areas which are not listed in Schedule 5 or section 29, *i.e.* the devolved areas. Not only that, it has power to amend or repeal existing Acts of the UK Parliament which relate to devolved matters. In addition, it should also be noted that the Scottish Ministers also have extensive powers to take decisions in areas where the Parliament itself does not have legislative competence. These powers may arise from "executive devolution", or from specific powers given to them in other Acts of the UK Parliament besides the Scotland Act.[6] Although, strictly speaking, Scottish Ministers will not be accountable to the Scottish Parliament when exercising powers derived in such ways, as the Parliament has the undoubted power to debate even non-devolved matters, it can be expected that the actions of Scottish Ministers in the exercise of such powers will be scrutinised by the Parliament, and it would be hard to see how a Scottish Executive (or individual Minister) which used such powers against the wishes of a majority of the Parliament could survive in office.

---

[6]See Chapter 6 for a discussion of executive devolution.

DEVOLVED MATTERS

Broadly speaking, the devolved areas are as follows:

Health

- overall responsibility for the NHS in Scotland including terms and conditions of service; public and mental health; education and training of health professionals.

Education and training

- pre-five, primary and secondary school education; teacher supply, training and conditions of service; the functions of Her Majesty's Inspectorate of Schools;
- further and higher education policy and funding, the functions of the Scottish Higher Education Funding Council; student support;
- science and research funding in support of devolved matters;
- training policy; vocational qualifications; careers advice and guidance.

Local government, social work and housing

- local government finance and local taxes;
- social work including children's hearings and the voluntary sector;
- housing including the functions of Scottish Homes;
- land-use planning; building control; area regeneration including the designation of enterprise zones.

Economic development and transport

- the functions of Scottish Enterprise, Highlands and Islands Enterprise and local enterprise companies;
- financial assistance to industry subject to UK guidelines; inward investment including the functions of Locate in Scotland;
- promotion of trade and exports;
- promotion of tourism including the functions of the Scottish Tourist Board;
- passenger and road transport; the Scottish road network; road safety; bus policy and concessionary fares; taxis and mini-cabs; some rail grant powers; the Strathclyde Passenger Transport Authority;
- air and sea transport covering ports, harbours and piers; freight shipping and ferry services; Highlands and Islands Airports Ltd; planning and environmental issues relating to airports;
- inland waterways.

Law and home affairs

- criminal law and procedure except for statutory offences relating to reserved matters including drugs and firearms;
- civil law except in relation to reserved matters;
- judicial appointments;
- the criminal justice and prosecution system;
- civil and criminal courts; tribunals concerned with devolved matters and the Scottish Council on Tribunals; legal aid;
- parole, the release of life prisoners, and alleged miscarriages of justice;
- prisons, the Scottish Prison Service; the treatment of offenders;
- police and fire services; civil defence and emergency planning;
- liquor licensing;
- protection of animals, domestic, captive and wild; zoo licensing; the control of dangerous wild animals and game.

Environment

- environmental protection; air, land and water pollution, and the functions of the Scottish Environmental Protection Agency; water supplies and sewerage; sustainable development policies within a UK framework;
- the natural heritage, countryside issues, the functions of Scottish National Heritage;
- the built heritage, and the functions of Historic Scotland;
- flood prevention, coast protection, and the safety of reservoirs.

Agriculture, forestry and fishing

- domestic agriculture including crofting; animal and plant health and animal welfare within a UK framework; implementation of measures under the Common Agricultural Policy;
- food standards;
- forestry including the Forestry Commission;
- domestic fisheries including inshore sea, salmon and freshwater fisheries and aquaculture; implementation of measure under the Common Fisheries Policy.

Sport and the arts

- sport and the functions of the Scottish Sports Council;
- the arts and the functions of the National Library, National Museums, and National Galleries of Scotland; the Scottish Museums Council, the Scottish Arts Council, Scottish Screen, and support for Gaelic.

Miscellaneous

- statistics, public registers and records including the responsibilities of the Keeper of the Records, the Keeper of the
  Registers and the Registrar General for Scotland.

THE POWER TO AMEND ACTS OF THE UK PARLIAMENT AND SCHEDULE 4

The Scottish Parliament has the power to amend or repeal Acts of the
UK Parliament which relate to devolved matters. There are, however,
limits placed on this power.[7] These are detailed in Schedule 4 which is
entitled "Enactments etc. protected from modification".

The Scottish Parliament cannot modify Articles 4 and 6 of the Acts
of Union of 1706/7 so far as they relate to freedom of trade. Nor can it
modify various sections of the European Communities Act 1972, the
Act by means of which the UK joined the European Communities.
The Human Rights Act 1998 which incorporates much of the European Convention on Human Rights is protected in its entirety from
modification by the Scottish Parliament. The law on reserved matters
cannot be modified and "law" is defined as including not only Acts
and subordinate legislation of the UK Parliament, but also any rule
of law which is not contained in an enactment the subject-matter of
which is a reserved matter. This protects common law rules relating
to reserved matters.

Significantly, the entire Scotland Act 1998, apart from a few
provisions, is protected from amendment. Most of the exceptions are
relatively minor, but they also include section 70, which deals with
accounts and audit, and section 91, which deals with the investigation
of complaints of maladministration.

---

[7]Section 29(2).

3. ELECTIONS AND MEMBERS

INTRODUCTION

The Scotland Act 1998 established the Scottish Parliament with 129 members elected by the form of proportional representation known as the additional member system.[1] This combines the relative majority system, commonly known as "first past the post", involving single member constituencies, with an additional element which "tops up" the political parties' representation from registered party lists by allocating regional seats on the basis of a second vote cast not for an individual but for a political party. It is also possible for individuals without any political affiliation to stand as candidates. Thus there are "constituency members" and "regional members". The Scotland Act refers to them simply as "members" but the term "MSP" has become the normal way in which they are described and, in law, the status of constituency and regional members is the same.

THE NUMBER OF MSPs

At the first general election to the Scottish Parliament in May 1999, 73 constituency members and 56 regional members were elected, the latter divided equally amongst eight regions. The Scotland Act specifies that the Orkney Islands and the Shetland Islands are to form separate constituencies. (These two island groups are combined into a single constituency for the purpose of elections to the Westminster Parliament.) The other constituencies for the Scottish Parliament are identical to the constituencies used for elections to the Westminster Parliament and will change as and when there are changes to those constituencies. At present, the electorate of a Scottish constituency is, on average, less than that of an English constituency because of a statutory requirement that there should be a minimum of 71 parliamentary constituencies in Scotland.[2] As a concession to the feeling that such relative over-representation at Westminster could no longer be justified once the Scottish Parliament had been established, the Scotland Act removes that minimum with the result that the size of the electorates in the parliamentary constituencies will become more in line with the size of those in England.[3] At the current populations for Scotland and England, this could mean that the number of

---

[1] See sections 1–18 of the Scotland Act 1998 for the provisions relating to MSPs and elections.

[2] In 1997, Scotland had an average of 55,339 electors per constituency while England had an average of 69,578 electors per constituency.

[3] Section 86.

parliamentary constituencies might be reduced by around 14 or 15 seats. However, the Boundary Commission for Scotland is required to give due weight to geographical considerations and local ties which might allow Scotland to have a slightly larger number of constituencies than it would otherwise be entitled to. Nevertheless, it seems inevitable that the consequence of the removal of a minimum number of parliamentary constituencies in Scotland will be that, in due course, the number of constituencies for the Scottish Parliament will be reduced to a figure in the region of 60. This reduction will come about after the Boundary Commission reports on the boundaries of parliamentary constituencies in Scotland, between 2002 and 2006. It is unlikely that the reduction will take effect for the second general election to the Scottish Parliament which must take place no later than 2003. It is probable, however, that the change in the number of constituencies will take effect for the next Scottish general election thereafter.

As the Boundary Commission is required, so far as is reasonably practicable, to keep the ratio of regional member seats to constituency seats the same as in the original arrangement, i.e. 56 to 73, this could mean that the number of regional member seats could fall to around 46. As the Scotland Act lays down that there must be eight regions, the number of regional members will fall to five or six per region.

It should be said, however, that the way in which the Scotland Act seeks to deal with the issue of Scottish representation at Westminster does not guarantee that such over-representation might not arise again in the future.[4] Furthermore, although the reduction in the number of MPs for Scottish constituencies at Westminster addresses one apparent anomaly produced by devolution in the constitutional arrangement of the UK as a whole, it does not meet the central issue raised by the "West Lothian Question",[5] namely the question as to whether it is acceptable for the MPs for Scottish constituencies at Westminster to make laws for England on subjects on which they are unable to legislate for Scotland as such subjects now fall within the remit of the Scottish Parliament. That question has led to increasing debate about the implications of devolution to Scotland and Wales for constitutional arrangements for England, in which numerous proposals have been put forward, ranging from regional government for England, the establishment of an English Grand Committee to the setting up of a fully-fledged parliament for England.

CONSTITUENCY AND REGIONAL MEMBERS

In the single-member constituencies, the successful candidate is the one who receives the most votes on the straightforward "first past

---

[4]In this, see John Curtice, "Reinventing the Yo-Yo? A Comment on the Electoral Provisions of the Scotland Bill" in "Scottish Affairs", No 23, Spring 1998, p 41.

[5]Named after the Labour MP for West Lothian and later Linlithgow, Tam Dalyell, who frequently raised this issue after devolution for Scotland was proposed in the 1970s.

the post" basis which currently applies in both local council and Westminster elections. Such constituency members are essentially elected as individuals although, in practice, most stand as the candidate of a political party. In the first general election to the Scottish Parliament, in May 1999, 72 of the 73 constituency members were candidates of political parties.[6]

Seven regional members were elected in each of eight Scottish regions. In the first general election, the boundaries of each region were the same as the 1996 boundaries for European Parliamentary constituencies. However, the choice of the European constituency as the basis for a region for the election of the regional members of the Scottish Parliament is purely a matter of administrative convenience; there is no link between the MSPs and the European constituency. Any link would have become superfluous with the abolition of constituencies for individual members of the European Parliament which took effect in 1999. When the number of regional members changes as a result of a change in the number of constituencies, the boundaries of the regions will no longer have any connection with the former European Parliamentary constituency boundaries.

In each region a registered political party[7] may submit a list of candidates for election as regional members. Each list may have up to twelve names on it (this allows for the filling of any vacancies which may arise from time to time). In addition, an individual without a party political affiliation may stand as an individual candidate as a regional member.

The Scotland Act permits a person to stand for election both as a constituency member (in only one constituency) and as a regional member provided that the constituency lies within the region concerned. The political parties used this as a fall-back mechanism in the first Scottish general election. Donald Dewar, the leader of the Labour Party in Scotland, stood as the Labour candidate in the Anniesland constituency in Glasgow. He was also at the top of the Labour Party's regional list for Glasgow to ensure that he was elected to the Parliament even if defeated in the Anniesland constituency.[8] The leaders of the Scottish Conservative Party, the Scottish National Party and the Scottish Socialist Party adopted the same belt and braces approach.[9]

---

[6]Dennis Canavan, the Labour MP for Falkirk West at Westminster, was deemed by his party to be "not good enough" to stand for the Scottish Parliament as an official Labour candidate. He stood as an independent in Falkirk West and won the seat with 54.98% of the votes cast.

[7]i.e. registered in terms of the Registration of Political Parties Act 1998.

[8]The official party reason for putting the leader of the party at the top of the regional list, as well as having him stand as a constituency member, was to maximise the regional vote for the party by having a well-known name at the top of the party list.

[9]The leaders of the Scottish Conservative Party and the Scottish Socialist Party failed to win constituency seats but were elected as regional members. The leaders of the Labour Party and the Scottish National Party were elected as constituency members. The leader of the Scottish Liberal Democrats, Jim Wallace, did not appear to have the same doubts as to his ability to win a constituency seat. His confidence was justified as he won 67.39% of the votes cast in the Orkney constituency, the highest personal vote of any candidate in the election.

Although it is unlikely that anyone would be nominated by more than one political party or stand both as a party candidate and as an individual candidate, there are provisions in the Scotland Act to ensure that this is not possible.[10]

At a general election for the Scottish Parliament, each voter has two votes. One vote is cast to choose a named candidate from those standing in that voter's constituency to be the constituency member. The other vote is cast to elect regional members. It may be cast either for the list submitted in that region by a registered political party or for an individual who is standing for election as a regional member. The voter, however, cannot choose to vote for a particular candidate on a party list; if he or she wishes to vote for the party list, he or she must do so *en bloc*. This type of list is known as a "closed" list.

In an attempt to avoid confusion, the ballot papers for the constituency seats in the first general election to the Scottish Parliament were lilac, while the ballot papers for the regional seats were peach-coloured. The local council elections were held on the same day as the first election to the Parliament and the ballot papers for these elections were white. Despite the efforts to avoid confusion, the counting of the votes was protracted, particularly in Lothian region, and final results were not known until late on the day following the elections.

THE ALLOCATION OF SEATS

The votes cast for the constituency candidates are counted first and the candidate who secures the majority of votes in each constituency is declared to be the MSP for that constituency. The reason that the constituency seats are decided first is because the regional member seats are allocated on the basis of correcting imbalances brought about by the "first past the post" system used in the constituency seats. If a party secures fewer constituency seats than its overall electoral support would suggest, it is allocated more of the regional seats to bring about a result in which the total number of seats won by any party is more proportional to the total number of votes cast for it in each region.

The calculation of the regional figures and the allocation of the regional seats is somewhat complex and the reader should refer to the attached table for an example of the calculation. For each political party which has submitted a list of candidates, the total number of regional votes cast throughout the region is divided by the number of constituency seats won by that party plus one. The resulting figure is called the "regional figure". Parties which did not gain any constituency seats are also involved in this calculation. Each time a party gains a regional member seat, that party's regional figure is recalculated. The regional figure for individual candidates is the total number of votes cast for the individual in all the constituencies included in the region.

---

[10]Section 5(7) and (8).

The first regional member seat is allocated to the party or individual with the highest regional figure. This will not necessarily be the party with the highest total of regional votes as account is taken of the number of constituency seats already won by the parties. The second and subsequent seats are then allocated on the basis of the recalculated regional figures. Seats are allocated to the persons on a party's list in the order in which they appear on the list, disregarding, of course, anyone who has already won a constituency seat.

In calculating the allocation of regional seats, account is taken only of the number of votes cast for the regional lists. A party which received a total of votes in the election of constituency members which varied substantially from the total of the votes cast for their regional list would not have that difference taken into account in the allocation of the additional seats from the regional list.

It can be seen from the example in the attached table that the system for allocating seats does in broad terms result in an allocation of seats in proportion to the number of votes cast for the candidates on the regional lists. It does not, however, result in complete proportionality. In percentage terms, the Scottish National Party, the Scottish Conservative Party, the Scottish Liberal Democrats and the Scottish Socialist Party received fewer seats in total than their shares of the regional votes, whereas the Labour Party received more seats than their share of the regional vote might otherwise have warranted.

It should be noted that an automatic side-effect of the eventual reduction in the number of regional members elected to the Parliament is that the likelihood that the allocation of seats (constituency and regional seats together) in a region will reflect in a proportionate way the number of votes cast for each party in that region will be reduced. The reason for this is that a reduced number of seats means that if one party gets more than its fair share of constituency seats there will be fewer regional seats available to correct that imbalance.

ELECTIONS

MSPs elected from both constituencies and regional lists are normally elected at the same time in a Scotland-wide general election. The first of these was held on 6th May 1999. The term of office of a Member of the Scottish Parliament begins on the day on which the Member is declared to be returned and ends with the dissolution of the Parliament. Subsequent ordinary general elections will take place on the first Thursday in May four years after the previous general election, with some flexibility being provided in that an ordinary general election can be held within a period running from one month before until one month after the first Thursday in May.

Extraordinary general elections can take place earlier than four years after the previous election in two situations. An extraordinary general election must be held if either a majority of MSPs amounting to not less than two-thirds of the total number of the seats in the

Parliament vote for an earlier election, or if the Parliament cannot agree on a nomination for the First Minister. The first situation therefore would arise only if a clear majority of the political parties represented in the Parliament wanted to hold an earlier general election, and a sufficient majority would probably require the support of three of the major political party groups. The requirement for a two-thirds majority thus makes it impossible for a government with a small majority to call an early general election at a time which it considered might suit its party political interests. This is in contrast to the situation in the UK Parliament which does not have a fixed term and the Prime Minister can call a general election at a time which suits him.

However, in the case of a failure to agree on the nomination of the First Minister, an early general election may arise as a result of a simple majority of MSPs voting against a nomination. If an extraordinary general election is held as a result of such a failure to agree on a nomination, and there continued thereafter to be no agreement on the nomination of a First Minister, extraordinary general elections could continue to be held. However, it might be expected that, in practice, such a situation would not develop, as the political parties held responsible for such repeat elections might fear that they would become unpopular as a result.

In the case of a seat falling vacant between elections, different mechanisms apply depending on whether the seat was previously held by a constituency member or a regional member. If the seat of a constituency member falls vacant for any reason such as death or resignation a by-election in the constituency will be held, normally within three months, to elect a replacement. However, if the latest date for holding the by-election would bring it within three months of the next ordinary election to the Parliament, the vacancy will remain unfilled until the next general election. This is to avoid the expense of the election process for the sake of filling the seat for only a few months. If the seat of a regional member falls vacant, different procedures apply depending on whether the seat was previously held by a member elected from a party list or a member who had been elected as an individual member. In the former case, the vacancy will be filled by the next person on that party's list who is willing to serve. In the latter case, the vacancy remains unfilled until the next general election.

The first by-election was brought about by the resignation, for family reasons, in December 1999, of the constituency member for Ayr. The by-election was held in March 2000 and was won by the Conservative candidate, thus giving the Conservatives their first constituency seat. This has no effect on the allocation of regional seats which remains fixed until the next general election in 2003.

Miscellaneous matters

The right to vote in elections to the Scottish Parliament is based on similar principles to the right to vote in elections to the UK Parliament. However it is extended to those who are entitled to vote in local government elections. The effect of this is to extend the right to vote to members of the House of Lords and to citizens of the Member States of the European Union who are resident in Scotland.[11]

The rules relating to disqualification from membership of the Scottish Parliament are similar to those for the House of Commons. Thus judges, civil servants (including the staff of the Scottish Executive), members of the armed forces, members of police forces and members of foreign legislatures are disqualified. Holders of certain public offices, for example members of Scottish Enterprise, Scottish Homes and the Crofters Commission, are also disqualified. However, members of the House of Lords (apart from the Law Lords), who are disqualified from membership of the House of Commons, are not ineligible to be MSPs merely because they are peers.[12] Three members of the House of Lords were elected as MSPs in the first general election in 1999.[13] Persons who are ordained and ministers of religion, many of whom are disqualified from standing for election to the House of Commons, are also eligible to stand for the Scottish Parliament as are citizens of the European Union who are resident in Scotland.

The date for the first general election on 6th May 1999 was set by the Secretary of State for Scotland and he continues to have the power to make rules for the conduct of elections, including rules on the procedure for electoral registration and on election expenses for both candidates and political parties. This power is exercised by the use of secondary legislation, which in this particular case requires the approval of both Houses of the Westminster Parliament.[14]

The Labour and Liberal Democrat representatives on the Scottish Constitutional Convention[15] came to an informal agreement that they would attempt to field an equal number of male and female candidates in winnable seats. Although some wanted this to be put into the Scotland Act, this was not done on the ground that it might fall foul of anti-sex discrimination legislation.[16] In their procedures for the selection of candidates for the constituency seats, the Labour Party "twinned" pairs of constituencies in most of Scotland and instructed their members to select one man and one woman candidate for each pair. There was no challenge to this from within the Labour Party.

---

[11]The fact that citizens of the European Union resident in Scotland were entitled to vote was misunderstood by some polling clerks in the first general election to the Scottish Parliament in 1999. As a result several EU citizens were denied the vote to which they were entitled.

[12]At the time of the first election to the Scottish Parliament, all peers were disqualified from standing for election to the House of Commons. With the passing of the House of Lords Act in November 1999, only those peers who remain as members of the House of Lords are so disqualified.

[13]Lord Steel (Liberal Democrat), Lord Watson (Labour), and Lord James Douglas-Hamilton (Conservative).

[14]Scotland Act 1998, s 12 and Schedule 7.

[15]For the Scottish Constitutional Convention, see Chapter 1.

[16]Prior to the 1997 general election, the Labour Party had attempted to increase the number of women MPs at Westminster by having all-women short lists. This was successfully challenged before an industrial tribunal by two male aspiring candidates. See *Jepson and Dyas-Elliot v The Labour Party* [1996] IRLR 116.

However, despite the agreement, the Liberal Democrats did not adopt such an approach as they were unable to get the agreement of their party to the proposal.

The Labour Party's procedures resulted in 28 men and 28 women being elected as Labour MSPs in the first general election in 1999. Of the Liberal Democrat MSPs elected in that election, 15 are men and only two are women. The comparable figures for the SNP are 20 men and 15 women, and for the Conservatives, 15 men and three women.

Dual mandates

Dual mandate is the term given to a situation where an individual is an elected member of two bodies and therefore has a mandate from two sets of electors. The Scotland Act does not prohibit dual mandates and thus it is possible for someone who is an MP in the UK Parliament, a Member of the European Parliament or a councillor to be elected as a member of the Scottish Parliament. In the first election to the Parliament in 1999, 15 serving MPs and three councillors were elected and did not resign their seats at Westminster or in their local councils.[17] There are, however, provisions which prevent an MSP who is also an MP or an MEP from drawing two full salaries[18] and a person who holds ministerial office in the UK government is not permitted to be a member of the Scottish Executive.[19] Westminster MPs, such as Donald Dewar and Henry McLeish, who held office in the UK government as Ministers in the Scottish Office, resigned from these posts on election to the Scottish Parliament.

THE RIGHTS AND OBLIGATIONS OF MSPs

MSPs are protected by what is called "absolute privilege" against any person seeking to take action against them on account of any statement made by them in proceedings of the Parliament. The publication of any statement made under the authority of the Parliament is similarly absolutely privileged.[20] As a result, they cannot be made to pay damages if such a statement is defamatory, even if the statement is made maliciously. The justification for this is that it is in the public interest for MSPs to be able to debate and discuss matters freely without any fear of being sued. This freedom of speech is somewhat similar to the freedom of speech enjoyed by MPs at Westminster. Unlike proceedings at Westminster, however, the

---

[17]Those members of the Scottish Parliament (especially those who are members of the Scottish Executive) who are also members of the UK Parliament find it difficult to attend meetings at Westminster and have come in for some criticism from opposition parties for poor attendance.

[18]See p 29.

[19]Scotland Act 1998, s 44 and see p 69.

[20]Scotland Act, s 41.

proceedings of the Scottish Parliament are subject to the law of contempt of court, except in respect of publications made in proceedings of the Parliament in relation to a Bill or subordinate legislation, or to the extent that a publication consists of a fair and accurate report of such proceedings made in good faith.[21] The Parliament's Standing Orders provide for a "sub judice" rule. This means that an MSP must not, in the proceedings of the Parliament, refer to any matter in relation to which legal proceedings are active, except to the extent permitted by the Presiding Officer, and if an MSP does refer to such a matter, the Presiding Officer may order that member not to do so.[22] However, nothing in this rule is to prevent the Parliament from legislating on any matter.

It should be noted that in any legal proceedings against the Parliament, a court may not make an order for interdict (or similar order) against the Parliament, but may make a declarator of the legal position instead.[23] The purpose of this is to afford the Parliament a measure of protection against attempts to interfere with its business through the use of legal proceedings. It is not yet clear what the consequences are for the Parliament of a declaratory order from a court.

Similarly, a court may not make an order for interdict (or similar order) against any MSP, the Presiding Officer or his deputies, or any member of staff of the Parliament in the Parliamentary corporation if the effect would be to give relief against the Parliament which could not have been given in proceedings against the Parliament. This provision is designed to prevent attempts to interfere with the business of the Parliament "by the back door".

As a result of a decision of the Court of Session early in 2000, it is, however, clear that, in certain circumstances, it is possible for a court to grant an interdict against an individual MSP.[24]

MSPs have certain obligations placed on them to ensure that they do not act in an improper manner. They, and their staff, are subject to the Prevention of Corruption Acts 1889 to 1916 which impose penalties for the corrupt making or acceptance of payments in money or in kind for activity in connection with the Parliament's business.[25]

The Scotland Act requires the Parliament to establish a register of members' interests, open to inspection by the public.[26] The initial rules relating to the register were made for the first members of the Scottish Parliament by a statutory instrument made by the Secretary of State for Scotland in May 1999. Every MSP must register any financial interest including benefits in kind and must declare that interest before taking part in any proceedings of the Parliament which relate to it. MSPs are also prohibited from advocating or initiating any cause, or urging another MSP to do so, for payment or for a benefit in

---

[21]Scotland Act, s 42.
[22]The Scottish Parliament's Standing Orders, Rule 7.5.
[23]Scotland Act, s 40 (3) and (4).
[24]*Whaley and others* v. *Lord Watson and the Scottish Parliamentary Corporate Body* 2000 GWD 8–269.
[25]Scotland Act, s 43.
[26]Scotland Act, s 39.

kind.[27] Any MSP who fails to declare an interest or who promotes a cause for payment is guilty of an offence and may be excluded from the Parliament. In addition, he or she may be prosecuted and, if found guilty, be liable to a fine. The Standing Orders of the Parliament require it to set up a number of committees which are called mandatory committees.[28] One of these is the Standards Committee and this committee must be established within 21 sitting days of a general election. The remit of the Standards Committee is to consider and report on the adoption, amendment and application of a Code of Conduct for MSPs and on whether the conduct of individual MSPs is in accordance with Standing Orders and with the Code of Conduct. The Standards Committee spent several months in the early days of the Parliament in the drafting of a detailed Code of Conduct.

However, one of the first tasks of the Standards Committee was to investigate claims made in a Sunday newspaper that a firm of lobbyists could guarantee access to Scottish Ministers. This became known as the "Lobbygate" affair. After interviewing various Ministers, their staff and members of the firm of lobbyists concerned, the members of the Standards Committee concluded that there was no truth in the allegations but an early priority for the committee became the regulation of the lobbying of the Parliament.

SALARIES

The Parliament is able to pay MSPs salaries, allowances and pensions[29] and the basic salary of each MSP, regardless of whether the member was elected as a constituency or a regional member, was set in the first year of the Parliament's existence at £40,092. Ministers receive an additional amount, depending on the level of seniority. The First Minister, for example, receives a ministerial allowance of £64,308.[30] If an MSP is also a member of the Westminster Parliament or of the European Parliament, he or she is entitled to receive the appropriate salary as well, but the Scottish Parliament must ensure that the element of salary which derives from membership of the Scottish Parliament is reduced.[31] The Parliament decided that the

---

[27]For an interesting example of a legal challenge to a MSP, alleging breach of the advocacy rule and acceptance of benefits in kind, see *Whaley and others* v. *Lord Watson and the Scottish Parliamentary Corporate Body* 2000 GWD 8–269. Lord Watson MSP introduced a member's Bill, the Protection of Wild Mammals Bill, the purpose of which was to ban foxhunting by dogs. He received legal and administrative assistance, including advice on drafting the Bill from the Scottish Campaign against Hunting with Dogs which the supporters of foxhunting considered to be benefits in kind.

The Inner House of the Court of Session decided that it had no power to prevent MSPs from breaching the members' interests rules. The rules can only be enforced by *retrospective* sanctions which include a fine.

[28]For the committees of the Parliament generally, see pp 37–41 below.

[29]Section 81.

[30]As a result of his dual mandate, the first First Minister, Donald Dewar, is entitled to earn more per annum than the Prime Minister of the UK. He elected to forgo his entitlement to one third of an MSP's salary.

[31]Section 82.

amount of the reduction should be two-thirds of the MSP's salary of £40,092. There is no reduction for MSPs who are also local authority councillors.

After every election each MSP is required to take the oath of allegiance to the Crown within a specified period (normally two months). Until the oath is taken, he or she cannot participate in the proceedings of the Parliament, or receive any payment of salary or allowances. If the oath is not taken within the specified period, the MSP concerned automatically loses his or her seat in the Parliament.[32] This provision concentrated the minds of various MSPs of a republican bent. They all took the oath of allegiance.

TABLE 1

Allocating seats on the regional list

1. In each region, the number of votes cast for each party in the 'second vote' for a regional list is totalled.
2. This total is then *divided* by the figure which equals **one plus** the number of **constituency members** elected for that party in that region.
3. The first regional seat is then allocated to the political party, or a candidate standing as an individual, having the highest figure after the calculation in step 2 above has been carried out.
4. The total votes cast for each party in the region are then divided by the figure which equals **one plus** the number of **constituency** *and* **regional members** elected for that party in that region. Where the calculation results in a number which is not a whole number, that number may be rounded down to the nearest whole number by the exercise of the returning officer's discretion.
5. The next regional seat is then allocated to the political party, or candidate standing as an individual, now having the highest figure after the calculation in step 4 above has been carried out.
6. This process of recalculation of the figure for each party is then carried out until all seven places for regional members have been allocated.
7. Seats on the regional list are allocated to candidates in the order in which the political parties have placed them on the list prior to the election.

The following example shows how the system of allocation of seats was carried out in Glasgow. There are ten constituency seats and seven regional seats in Glasgow.

1. The number of individual constituency members elected was as follows:

---

[32]Sections 83, 84.

Scottish Conservative and Unionist Party	0
Scottish Labour Party	10
Scottish Liberal Democrats	0
Scottish National Party	0
Scottish Socialist Party	0
Others	0

2. The number of regional list votes cast was as follows:

Communist Party of Great Britain	521
Humanist Party	447
Natural Law Party (Scotland)	419
Prolife Alliance	2,357
Scottish Conservative and Unionist Party	20,239
Scottish Green Party	10,159
Scottish Labour Party	112,588
Scottish Liberal Democrats	18,473
Scottish National Party	65,360
Scottish Socialist Party	18,581
Scottish Unionist Party	2,283
Socialist Labour Party	4,391
Socialist Party of Great Britain	309
Bridget McGeechan, Independent Choice	221

3. **The first seat**   The above totals were then divided by the figure of one plus the number of constituency members elected for each party to give the regional figure for each. As the Scottish Labour Party was the only party to win any seats, their figure of 112,588 is divided by 11 (10+1). The other parties' figures are divided by 1 (0+1) and therefore their regional figures are the same as in the table above. The winning party is marked*

Communist Party of Great Britain	521
Humanist Party	447
Natural Law Party (Scotland)	419
Prolife Alliance	2,357
Scottish Conservative and Unionist Party	20,239
Scottish Green Party	10,159
Scottish Labour Party	10,235
Scottish Liberal Democrats	18,473
Scottish National Party	65,360*
Scottish Socialist Party	18,581
Scottish Unionist Party	2,283
Socialist Labour Party	4,391
Socialist Party of Great Britain	309
Bridget McGeechan, Independent Choice	221

As a result of this calculation, the SNP had the highest regional figure so the top person on its regional list was elected. Thus, the total number of MSPs elected for each party at that stage was as follows:

Scottish Labour Party   10
Scottish National Party   1
Others   0

4. **The second seat**   Since the SNP had won the first seat, their regional figure was recalculated by dividing their original regional figure by 2 (1+1), giving the following:

Communist Party of Great Britain	521
Humanist Party	447
Natural Law Party (Scotland)	419
Prolife Alliance	2,357
Scottish Conservative and Unionist Party	20,239
Scottish Green Party	10,159
Scottish Labour Party	10,235
Scottish Liberal Democrats	18,473
Scottish National Party	32,680* (ie 65,360 ÷ 2)
Scottish Socialist Party	18,581
Scottish Unionist Party	2,283
Socialist Labour Party	4,391
Socialist Party of Great Britain	309
Bridget McGeechan, Independent Choice	221

Since the regional figure for the SNP was still higher than the figure for any other party, the second person on the SNP's regional list was elected. Thus, the total number of MSPs elected for each Party was as follows:

Scottish Labour Party   10
Scottish National Party   2
Others   0

5. **The third seat**   The SNP's regional figure was calculated again. The SNP's original regional figure was now divided by 3 (2+1), giving the following figures:

Communist Party of Great Britain	521
Humanist Party	447
Natural Law Party (Scotland)	419
Prolife Alliance	2,357
Scottish Conservative and Unionist Party	20,239
Scottish Green Party	10,159
Scottish Labour Party	10,235
Scottish Liberal Democrats	18,473
Scottish National Party	21,786* (ie 65,360 ÷ 3)
Scottish Socialist Party	18,581
Scottish Unionist Party	2,283
Socialist Labour Party	4,391
Socialist Party of Great Britain	309

Bridget McGeechan, Independent Choice   221

The regional figure for the SNP was still higher than the figure for any other party, so the third person on the SNP's list was elected. The figures for the parties are now as follows:

Scottish Labour Party   10
Scottish National Party   3
Others   0

6. **The fourth seat**   The SNP's regional figure was recalculated. This time the SNP's original regional figure was divided by 4 (3+1). The following figures resulted:

Communist Party of Great Britain	521
Humanist Party	447
Natural Law Party (Scotland)	419
Prolife Alliance	2,357
Scottish Conservative and Unionist Party	20,239*
Scottish Green Party	10,159
Scottish Labour Party	10,235
Scottish Liberal Democrats	18,473
Scottish National Party	16,340 (ie 65,360 ÷ 4)
Scottish Socialist Party	18,581
Scottish Unionist Party	2,283
Socialist Labour Party	1,391
Socialist Party of Great Britain	309
Bridget McGeechan, Independent Choice	221

The party which now had the highest figure was the Scottish Conservative and Unionist Party and therefore the person at the top of their list was elected. The numbers of seats for the parties were then as follows:

Scottish Labour Party   10
Scottish National Party   3
Scottish Conservative and Unionist Party   1

7. **The fifth seat**   This time the regional figure for the Scottish Conservative and Unionist Party is recalculated by being divided by 2 (1+1). This resulted in the following figures:

Communist Party of Great Britain	521	
Humanist Party	447	
Natural Law Party (Scotland)	419	
Prolife Alliance	2,357	
Scottish Conservative and Unionist Party	10,119	(i.e. 20,239 ÷ 2 and rounded down to the nearest whole number)
Scottish Green Party	10,159	

Scottish Labour Party	10,235
Scottish Liberal Democrats	18,473
Scottish National Party	16,340
Scottish Socialist Party	18,581*
Scottish Unionist Party	2,283
Socialist Labour Party	4,391
Socialist Party of Great Britain	309
Bridget McGeechan, Independent Choice	221

The party which now had the highest regional figure was the Scottish Socialist Party and so the person at the top of their list was elected. The number of seats for the parties was then as follows:

Scottish Labour Party	10
Scottish National Party	3
Scottish Conservative and Unionist Party	1
Scottish Socialist Party	1

8. **The sixth seat**   This time the Scottish Socialist Party's regional figure was recalculated by being divided by 2 (1+1). This resulted in the following figures:

Communist Party of Great Britain	521
Humanist Party	447
Natural Law Party (Scotland)	419
Prolife Alliance	2,357
Scottish Conservative and Unionist Party	10,119
Scottish Green Party	10,159
Scottish Labour Party	10,235
Scottish Liberal Democrats	18,473*
Scottish National Party	16,340
Scottish Socialist Party	9,290 (ie 18,581 ÷ 2 and rounded down to the nearest whole number)
Scottish Unionist Party	2,283
Socialist Labour Party	4,391
Socialist Party of Great Britain	309
Bridget McGeechan, Independent Choice	221

The party with the highest figure was the Scottish Liberal Democrats and so the person at the top of their list was elected. The seats for the parties were thus:

Scottish Labour Party	10
Scottish National Party	3
Scottish Conservative and Unionist Party	1
Scottish Socialist Party	1
Scottish Liberal Democrats	1

9. **The seventh seat** The last recalculation was carried out. The Scottish Liberal Democrats regional figure was divided by 2 (1+1). The figures are as follows:

Communist Party of Great Britain	521
Humanist Party	447
Natural Law Party (Scotland)	419
Prolife Alliance	2,357
Scottish Conservative and Unionist Party	10,119
Scottish Green Party	10,159
Scottish Labour Party	10,235
Scottish Liberal Democrats	9,236 (ie 18,473 ÷ 2 and rounded down to the nearest whole number)
Scottish National Party	16,340*
Scottish Socialist Party	9,290.5
Scottish Unionist Party	2,283
Socialist Labour Party	4,391
Socialist Party of Great Britain	309
Bridget McGeechan, Independent Choice	221

The party with the highest regional figure was the Scottish National Party, so the person next on their list was elected to the seventh and last regional seat.

The number of seats won as both constituency and regional members can now be contrasted with the percentage of votes cast on the regional list as follows:

PARTY	FPTP SEATS WON	REGIONAL SEATS WON	TOTAL SEATS WON	% OF REGIONAL VOTES	% OF SEATS WON
Labour	10	0	10	43.9	58.82
SNP	0	4	4	25.5	23.54
Con	0	1	1	7.9	5.88
Sc. Soc.	0	1	1	7.2	5.88
Lib Dems	0	1	1	7.2	5.88
Green	0	0	0	4.0	0
Soc. Lab.	0	0	0	1.7	0
Prolife	0	0	0	0.9	0
Sc. Unionist	0	0	0	0.9	0
Communist	0	0	0	0.2	0
Humanist	0	0	0	0.2	0
Nat. Law	0	0	0	0.2	0
SPGB	0	0	0	0.1	0
Independent	0	0	0	0.1	0

4. HOW THE PARLIAMENT WORKS

INTRODUCTION

The supporters of the establishment of a Scottish Parliament frequently expressed the hope that such a body would be a new type of institution, with a new approach to the way that the business of government is carried on.[1] This chapter looks at the way in which that hope has been reflected in the reality of the arrangements made for the way the Parliament works. It considers in some detail the role of the Parliament's committees. It also looks at the opportunities that are available to MSPs to hold the Scottish Administration to account, and the way in which external individuals and organisations can influence the Parliament's work.

THE LEGISLATIVE FRAMEWORK

The Parliament is given a relatively free hand by the Scotland Act in deciding how it should work. The Act does not set out detailed requirements for the Parliament's method of operation. It states that the proceedings of the Parliament will be regulated by standing orders.[2] Beyond that general requirement, there are only a small number of areas where the Act specifies what should be in the standing orders.

These statutory requirements contain important provisions about the passage of legislation, including procedures to ensure that the Parliament cannot make legislation on matters which are outside the powers given to it. These provisions are considered in the next chapter.

There are a number of other specific matters which the Scotland Act requires the Parliament to deal with in its standing orders, including rules to provide for the following[3]:

- the preservation of order in the Parliament's proceedings, including the prevention of criminal conduct or contempt of court during proceedings, and the prevention of the discussion of matters which are *sub judice*;
- that the proceedings of the Parliament are to be held in public, except in certain specified circumstances;
- provision that the Presiding Officer and his or her deputies are not all to come from the same political party;

---

[1] See, for example, Bernard Crick and David Millar, *To Make the Parliament of Scotland a Model for Democracy* (John Wheatley Centre, 1997).
[2] Section 22.
[3] Schedule 3.

- that any committees and sub-committees which are set up must take account of the balance of seats held by the different political parties in the Parliament.

The standing orders may also include rules allowing for the exclusion of MSPs from sittings of the Parliament and its committees and sub-committees, in certain circumstances.

It can be seen, therefore, that the Act only lays down broad guidelines for the operation of the Parliament, and in particular for how proposals for legislation should pass through the Parliament. The Act does not set out detailed guidelines for the way in which committees should operate, or for the number of readings that proposed legislation should pass through in the Parliament.

STANDING ORDERS

However, although the statutory requirements to be observed by the Parliament in deciding how it should function are relatively few, the Parliament operates within the framework of a comprehensive set of Standing Orders. In order that the Parliament would have Standing Orders in force when it commenced operation, its first Standing Orders were put in place by the Secretary of State for Scotland,[4] using his powers to make transitional provisions for the Parliament. These were superseded when the Parliament adopted its own Standing Orders in December 1999, although in fact these are virtually identical to its initial "transitional" Standing Orders. The Parliament may, on a motion made by its Procedures Committee, amend its Standing Orders, if an absolute majority of MSPs so decide.[5]

The Standing Orders are modelled largely, although not completely, on the proposals made by the Consultative Steering Group on the Scottish Parliament (the "CSG"). The CSG was set up by the UK Government early in 1998 to make proposals as to how the Parliament should carry out its business. It drew together representatives of all the major political parties along with other leading constitutional experts, and published its final report, *Shaping Scotland's Parliament*, in January 1999.[6] Its broad recommendations were endorsed by all the major political parties.

THE COMMITTEES OF THE PARLIAMENT

In most legislative assemblies, much of the detailed work is dealt with in committees rather than in a plenary session of all the body's members. The arrangements for an assembly's committee structure

---

[4]These can be found in the Schedule to SI 1999/1095, *The Scotland Act 1998 (Transitory and Transitional Provisions) (Standing Orders and Parliamentary Publications) Order 1999.*

[5]Rule 17.1 of the *Standing Orders of the Scottish Parliament*. (Subsequent references to Rules are references to the rules set out in these Standing Orders.)

[6]The Stationery Office, 1999. Referred to elsewhere in this book as the "CSG Report".

are therefore a key aspect of its method of operation. This is particularly so in the case of the Scottish Parliament, where committees play a significant role in its activities. The basic model for its committee structure, in line with the recommendations of the CSG,[7] provides for all-purpose "subject" committees, which combine the roles of both standing and select committees in the Westminster model. The Standing Orders do not specify the remits of such subject committees, and it is up to the Parliament, on the proposal of either the Parliamentary Bureau or an individual MSP,[8] to decide from time to time which subject committees should be set up.

The CSG also proposed that the Parliament should be able to set up *ad hoc* committees to allow consideration of issues on a broad basis, in order to deal with matters which cut across the conventional boundaries of government (for example, public health, social inclusion, and environmental sustainability). The Standing Orders do not make specific provision for such *ad hoc* committees, but they are sufficiently flexible to allow the establishment of such committees if the Parliament so wishes. Moreover, the subject committees which were set up by the Parliament after its first elections in 1999 were given broad remits. Eight subject committees were established then: *Education, Culture & Sport; Enterprise & Lifelong Learning; Health & Community Care; Justice & Home Affairs; Local Government; Rural Affairs; Social Inclusion, Housing & Voluntary Sector; Transport & the Environment.*

Although the Standing Orders do not specify which subject committees should be established, they do require certain committees, described as "mandatory committees", to be set up. These are the Procedures Committee, the Standards Committee, the Finance Committee, the Audit Committee, the European Committee, the Equal Opportunities Committee, the Public Petitions Committee, and the Subordinate Legislation Committee.[9] In addition, the Parliament has to set up a Parliamentary Bureau.[10] Most of these committees are concerned with organisational and procedural matters, and a brief description of their remits is given below. (It will be noted that some of the mandatory committees, in particular the European and Equal Opportunities Committees, have remits which in fact allow them also to deal with certain wider policy areas, similar to those which are dealt with by subject committees.)

A committee may consider any matter which is within its specific remit, or any other matter which is referred to it by the full Parliament or by any other committee. Where a matter is within its remit, or is otherwise referred to it, a committee can undertake a number of activities.[11] It can:

- consider the policy and administration of the Scottish Administration;

---

[7]CSG Report at 2.9 *et seq.* and 3.2.58 *et seq.*
[8]Rule 6.1.
[9]Rule 6.1.5.
[10]Rule 5.1.
[11]See Rule 6.2.

- consider any proposals for legislation, including both primary or secondary legislation, whether before the Scottish Parliament or the UK Parliament;
- consider any relevant European Communities legislation or international agreements or the like;
- consider whether there is a need for law reform in a particular area;
- initiate Bills for consideration by the Parliament;
- consider the financial proposals and financial administration of the Scottish Administration.

Each committee has between five and 15 members. Members are appointed by the Parliament on a proposal from the Parliamentary Bureau.[12] Committees choose their own convener and deputy convener, but the Parliamentary Bureau recommends to the full Parliament the party from which they are to be appointed, and is required in so doing to take account of the proportionate strength of the various parties in the Parliament. Committees normally meet in public unless the committee decides otherwise: when considering actual or potential proposals for legislation, a committee must meet in public unless it is taking evidence when it can decide to meet in private. Committees can, with the approval of the Parliamentary Bureau and the full Parliament, establish their own sub-committees.[13]

Ministers are not barred from becoming members of committees, but as matter of practice have not been appointed to either subject or mandatory committees. However, a Minister does have the right to participate (but not vote) in proceedings of a committee concerning proposals for legislation in the relevant subject area (as does the individual member concerned in the case of a Member's Bill), and in practice Ministers will, on occasion, attend a relevant committee.

A committee may decide, with the approval of the Parliamentary Bureau, to sit anywhere in Scotland, and a number of meetings have been held outside Edinburgh. However, the vast majority of committee meetings are held within the Parliament's own headquarters building in Edinburgh, notwithstanding the recommendation of the CSG that some committees should be permanently based outside Edinburgh "to demonstrate that the Parliament is a Parliament for the whole of Scotland".[14]

Committees may appoint external advisers to assist them with their work,[15] although the CSG recommendation that non-MSPs could be co-opted onto committees as non-voting members has not been incorporated into the Standing Orders. Committees may also appoint a "reporter" to report to it on any matter within its remit.[16] This would allow the Scottish Parliament to make use of the "rapporteur"

---

[12]Rule 6.3.1.

[13]See Chapter 12 of the Rules for the detailed provisions for Committee Procedures.

[14]Rule 12.3.2; CSG Information Paper CSG (98)(92).

[15]Rule 12.7. A number of committees have made use of the power to appoint advisers.

[16]Rule 12.6.

system extensively used in the European Parliament and elsewhere, where such a person draws up a draft report for a committee. It was envisaged by the CSG that a "rapporteur" would act as a focal point for interest groups and individuals wishing to make representations to a committee. Parliamentary committees have begun to make use of the power to appoint a reporter, although as yet, such an appointment does not seem to have acquired the influence which can be wielded by a "rapporteur" in the European system.

THE REMITS OF THE COMMITTEES

Each committee of the Parliament is given a specific area of responsibility, its "remit".[17] The remits of mandatory committees are set out in the Standing Orders. The remit of a subject committee is decided by the Parliamentary Bureau, subject to the approval of the full Parliament.

The remit of each committee is summarised as follows:

Subject Committees

- **Education, Culture & Sport** School and pre-school education; arts, culture and sport; built heritage and lottery funding.
- **Enterprise & Lifelong Learning** The Scottish economy; industry, tourism, trade and inward investment; higher and further education, lifelong learning and training; science matters; co-ordination of policy on Highlands and Islands, and Gaelic.
- **Health & Community Care** Health and community care issues.
- **Justice & Home Affairs** Administration of civil and criminal justice; reform of the civil and criminal law; social work; land reform policy; police, fire & emergency planning; illegal drugs; freedom of information.
- **Local Government** Local government matters generally.
- **Rural Affairs** Rural development; agriculture, fisheries and forestry.
- **Social Inclusion, Housing, & Voluntary Sector** Housing; the voluntary sector; social inclusion; equalities issues.
- **Transport & Environment** Transport and environment issues.

Mandatory Committees

- **Procedures** The practice and procedures of the Parliament.
- **Standards** The Code of Conduct for MSPs; allegations of breach of the Code; members' interests, and members' conduct in general. (If an MSP has breached the code, the committee can recommend to the Parliament that that

---

[17]See Rules, Chapter 6.

member's Parliamentary rights and privileges can be withdrawn for a specified period.)[18]

- **Finance** Consideration of the Executive's public expenditure proposals (including Budget Bills), any proposals to use the Parliament's tax-varying power, and any proposals from a committee concerning public expenditure.
- **Audit** Public expenditure accounts and reports from the Auditor General for Scotland.
- **European** Proposals for, and the implementation of, European Communities legislation; any other European issue concerning the Parliament.
- **Equal Opportunities Committee** Equal opportunities matters, both external and internal to the Parliament.
- **Public Petitions Committee** Initial consideration of public petitions, and what action should be taken as a result.
- **Subordinate Legislation Committee** Consideration of subordinate legislation, and in particular whether proposals raise certain specified issues of importance which the full Parliament should consider.[19]

The remit of the Parliamentary Bureau is considered below.

THE PARLIAMENTARY BUREAU

A particularly important role in the management of the Parliament's business is played by its Parliamentary Bureau. The Bureau operates under special rules set out in the Standing Orders, and although clearly a committee of the Parliament, it is not governed by the same rules that apply to other committees.[20] The Bureau is comprised of the Presiding Officer, and one representative of each party with five or more MSPs (nominated by the Parliamentary leader of that party). In addition, members of parties with fewer than five MSPs, or independents, can combine together to form a group of five or more members for the purpose of appointing a representative to the Bureau.[21] Members of the Bureau vote on a "weighted basis", where they wield one vote for each MSP their party has in the full Parliament.

The main functions of the Parliamentary Bureau are to:

- recommend to the Parliament its business programme;
- recommend the establishment, remit, membership, and duration of any committee or sub-committee of the Parliament;
- decide any issue as to whether a matter comes within the responsibility of a particular committee, and to decide which committee should be the "lead committee" where an issue falls within the responsibility of more than one committee.

---

[18]Rule 6.5.2.
[19]See Rules 6.11 and 10.3.1.
[20]See Rules, Chapter 5.
[21]This last provision was not utilised in the Parliament elected in 1999 as all but three MSPs were elected from the larger parties.

The Presiding Officer chairs meetings of the Bureau, but has no vote, unless there is a tie when he or she can use a casting vote. A deputy Presiding Officer chairs the meeting in the absence of the Presiding Officer. Meetings of the Bureau are held in private, although it can if it wishes invite other MSPs to participate in a meeting, on a non-voting basis.

HOLDING THE EXECUTIVE TO ACCOUNT

As well as making laws, most parliamentary assemblies have the important role of monitoring how governments implement the law once made, and how they carry out their functions in general. As with many other activities, the Scotland Act places no statutory require-ments on the Parliament as to how it should go about the task of holding the executive arm of government to account. However, reflecting a widely-held view that effective scrutiny of the Scottish Executive be incorporated into the practice of the Parliament, the CSG made detailed proposals on how such accountability could be put into effect.[22] The Standing Orders eventually adopted by the Parlia-ment are broadly based upon the CSG proposals, although they are not quite as comprehensive as envisaged by the CSG. The following opportunities to ensure such accountability are available to the Parliament:

- MSPs may ask both oral and written questions (oral questions have to be submitted in advance in writing, but supplemen-tary questions are allowed).[23]
- The First Minister may, if he or she so wishes, make a statement to the Parliament outlining the "proposed policy objectives and the legislative programme of the Scottish Executive" for the Parliamentary year ahead, and if such a statement is made it will be debated by the Parliament.[24] This provision is optional, however, rather than mandatory as the CSG seemed to suggest should be the case. (Neither was the CSG recommendation that after each election the Parliament should debate the four-year legislative programme of the newly formed Scottish Executive incorporated into the Stand-ing Orders, although such a debate was held after the Labour-Liberal Democrat coalition was formed in 1999.)
- Debates on general policy issues can be held from time to time, and a specified number of days are reserved for debates initiated by committees and opposition parties. Individual MSPs have an opportunity to raise items of business also.[25]
- A motion of no confidence in either the entire Scottish Executive or an individual Minister can be tabled by any MSP,

---

[22]CSG Report, 3.4.
[23]See Chapter 13 of the Rules on Statements and Parliamentary Questions.
[24]Rule 5.7
[25]Rule 5.6

and if it is supported by at least 25 members, it must be debated. (It would appear, however, that as the Scotland Act only provides for the resignation of the Scottish Executive *en bloc* following a no confidence vote, only a vote of no confidence in the entire Executive would be binding. A vote of no confidence in an individual Minister would seem to be advisory only (although no doubt such a vote would be most telling).)[26]

It was noted above that individual Ministers can participate in the work of a committee when considering that Minister's legislative proposals, and such participation was seen by the CSG as a further opportunity for committees to scrutinise the activity of the Scottish Executive.

THE PRESIDING OFFICER

It will be seen from other sections of this book that the Parliament's Presiding Officer plays an important part in its activities. Under the statutory provisions of the Scotland Act, he or she has a very important job to play in the procedure whereby proposed legislation passes through the Parliament.[27] The Standing Orders give further important responsibilities to the Presiding Officer.[28] These include the duty to:

- preside over plenary meetings of the Parliament;
- convene and chair the Parliamentary Bureau;
- interpret and apply the Standing Orders;
- represent the Parliament in discussions and exchanges with any parliamentary, governmental, administrative or other body, whether within or outwith the United Kingdom.

The Act provides that the Parliament will elect a Presiding Officer and two deputies, who must not all represent the same party.[29] The Standing Orders further provide that the Presiding Officer and the deputy Presiding Officers have casting votes in the event of a tie in a plenary meeting of the Parliament (except where there is a tie in a vote for First Minister, Presiding Officer and deputies, and members of the Parliamentary corporation), or in a meeting of the Parliamentary Bureau.[30] The Presiding Officer does not otherwise have a vote,[31]

---

[26]See Rule 8.12 and sections 45, 47, 48, and 49 of the Scotland Act 1998.
[27]See Chapter 5 below.
[28]See Chapter 3 of the Rules for the detailed provisions applicable to the Presiding Officer and deputy Presiding Officers.
[29]The Parliament elected a Liberal Democrat MSP as its first Presiding Officer, with Deputies from the Labour Party and the SNP.
[30]Rule 5.3.1.
[31]Rule 11.5.5.

but the deputies have normal voting rights except when actually presiding over Parliamentary business. To be appointed each of the Presiding Officer and deputies must obtain an absolute majority of those MSPs *actually voting in that election*,[32] but once appointed, can only be removed by an absolute majority of *all* MSPs.[33]

The Standing Orders specifically require the Presiding Officer and deputies when exercising their functions to "act impartially, taking account of the interests of all members equally".[34] Nevertheless, the functions of the posts have the potential, particularly in the case of the Presiding Officer, to give their holders considerable influence over the business of the Parliament. The degree to which that proves to be the case will no doubt depend on the personality of the person elected to the post, and the political balance between the parties represented in the Parliament. Given that the electoral system makes it likely that there will rarely be a party holding a clear majority of seats and that, accordingly, there will be a greater role for inter-party bargaining, there is a reasonable possibility that the post of Presiding Officer is one which will have, on a continuing basis, a public profile, and perhaps also degree of political influence, greater than its Westminster counterpart.

PUBLIC ACCOUNTABILITY

As outlined above, the key principles adopted by the CSG include an emphasis on the Parliament being open and accountable to the wider Scottish public. The only provision of the Act giving any rights to the public over the system of government in Scotland is that requiring the Parliament to set up a system to investigate complaints made by members of the public to MSPs alleging maladministration by members of the Scottish Executive, or any other member of the Scottish Administration (or any one acting on their behalf, including of course civil servants).[35] That provision is modelled on the existing UK Parliamentary Ombudsman system, and the obligation to set up such a system is restricted to complaints of the kind which that UK official is required to investigate (in essence, complaints of maladministration by government departments, but excluding a number of matters such as the investigation of crime and commercial transactions).[36]

However, the Act allows the Parliament, if it wishes, to set up a wider investigatory system, including amongst others the investigation of any action taken by or on behalf of the Scottish Parliamentary Corporate Body (see below), any action taken by or on behalf of any Scottish public authority with mixed functions or no reserved

---

[32]See Rule 11.9.
[33]Rule 3.5.
[34]Rule 3.1.3.
[35]Section 91.
[36]See Parliamentary Commissioner Act 1967, Sched. 3.

functions, and any action concerning Scotland, and not relating to reserved matters, which is taken by or on behalf of a cross-border public authority.[37] It appears to be open to the Parliament to decide whether or not complaints made under any such wider investigatory system would have to be made through MSPs, in contrast with the "Ombudsman" system which the Parliament has a legal duty to establish.

Initial arrangements for an Ombudsman for the Scottish Parliament were put in place by the Secretary of State for Scotland under his powers to make transitional arrangements under the Scotland Act.[38] These set up the office of Scottish Parliamentary Commissioner for Administration, with powers and procedures modelled very much on the existing counterpart at UK Parliamentary level. These transitional arrangements will continue in force until such time as the Scottish Parliament decides to set up its own arrangements for an Ombudsman. These transitional arrangements could therefore remain in place indefinitely. The Ombudsman appointed under these arrangements was the current UK Parliamentary Commissioner for Administration.

Beyond these provisions, the Act places no specific duties on the Parliament to ensure public accountability and openness. However, the CSG made recommendations in this area also. It envisaged that an important method open to members of the public who wished to bring matters to the attention of the Parliament would be a system for the consideration of petitions,[39] and the Standing Orders duly make provision for any member of the public, or organisation, to submit a petition on any matter of concern to the Parliament.[40] This system allows any member of the public to submit a written petition to the Parliament on any matter within its legislative competence. Such a petition can be submitted via an MSP, or directly by the individual concerned to the Parliament. There is no requirement that a certain minimum number of signatures be obtained in support of the petition (as is the norm in many assemblies elsewhere in Europe[41]). The petition is considered first by the Public Petitions Committee of the Parliament. Having considered whether the Parliament has the power to deal with the issue raised, the Committee can then deal with the petition in a number of ways. It can forward it to the Scottish Executive or other authority for information or consideration; refer it to the relevant subject committee; or prepare a report on the petition

---

[37]Section 91.

[38]The Scotland Act 1998 (Transitory and Transitional Provisions) (Complaints of Maladministration) Order 1999, SI 1999/1351.

[39]CSG Report, 3.6.13 et seq.

[40]Rules 15.4–15.6. In the first eight months of its operation, the Parliament considered more than 90 petitions, some it should be noted emanating from particularly active petitioners who lodged petitions on various different issues (in the case of at least one petitioner, causing the Public Petitions Committee some concern as to how it could deal with the volume of his petitions!).

[41]e.g. Germany and Italy. See Chapter 4 of the report, Parliamentary Practices in Devolved Parliaments (Centre for Scottish Public Policy for the Scottish Office, 1998).

for consideration and/or debate by the Parliament Plenary or take any other action it considers appropriate.

The CSG also emphasised that prior to legislation being submitted to the Parliament, there should be extensive consultation with organisations and individuals outside the Parliament. To achieve this, as mentioned below,[42] it recommended that legislative proposals from the Scottish Executive should be accompanied by a memorandum showing what public consultation has been undertaken, and the Standing Orders provide that such details must be included in a "Policy Memorandum".[43] The CSG also suggested that there might be a role for forums bringing together particular interest groups, e.g. a Civic Forum, a Business Forum, a Youth Forum.[44] To date, however, the Scottish Executive has only indicated that it will support the establishment of a Civic Forum. Proposals to fund the Civic Forum, which would initially receive funding of £100,000 per year, were announced by the Scottish Executive towards the end of 1999.

The wish to ensure that the Parliament is seen to represent "the whole of Scotland" is reflected in the provision in the Standing Orders that although the Parliament shall normally conduct its business in English, members may also speak in Scots Gaelic or in any other language with the agreement of the Presiding Officer.[45] However, although interpretation facilities are provided within the building, the Parliament does not have its own interpreters available on a permanent basis, and those wishing to speak in another language than English are required to give 24 hours' notice in order to ensure that interpreters can be provided. Moreover, there is no automatic provision for MSPs' speeches to be interpreted *into* English from Gaelic or any other language. Accordingly, it is not possible for languages other than English to be used on a day-to-day basis, and it may be thought that the provision to allow the use of Gaelic is more of symbolic significance rather than practical utility for the normal business of the Parliament. (The right to use Scots Gaelic only applies to speeches by MSPs. Public petitions, for example, are only admissible if they are in English.)[46]

The Parliament has also adopted the CSG recommendation that it should avoid the Westminster practice of Parliamentary sittings starting in the afternoon and running until late at night but rather follow what have been described as "family-friendly" hours of business. The Standing Orders lay down that the Parliament will normally sit on Monday afternoon, from Tuesday to Thursday between 9.30 am and 5.30 pm, and on Friday mornings. Moreover, the Parliamentary Bureau is obliged to take account of the dates of school holidays when considering what weeks the Parliament should be in recess.[47]

---

[42]See Chapter 5.
[43]Rule 9.3.3.(c)(ii).
[44]CSG Report, 2.38.
[45]Rule 7.1.1.
[46]Rule 15.4.3.
[47]Rule 2.2.

SCOTTISH PARLIAMENTARY CORPORATE BODY (SPCB)

A brief mention should be made of the SPCB, which is established by the Scotland Act.[48] The principal function of this body, described in the Parliament's Standing Orders as the "Parliamentary Corporation", is to provide the Parliament with the property, staff, and services it requires. This includes the staff who service committees, parliamentary researchers and librarians, and other ancillary staff. The SPCB is also responsible for the preparation of the Parliament's Official Report, its Official Journal. It also arranges for the broadcasting of the Parliament's proceedings, subject to a Code of Conduct set down by the full Parliament.[49] The establishment of the SPCB ensures that these services are provided independently of the Scottish Executive. The members of the SPCB, who direct its operation (subject to the Parliament's rights to give directions to it) are the Presiding Officer and four other MSPs. It was not envisaged by the CSG that these members would be appointed on a political basis but the Rules say nothing on this point, and in fact the four main parties in the Parliament agreed amongst themselves that they would each appoint one member of the SPCB when the first appointments to the body were made.

Any legal proceedings by or against the Parliament, its Presiding Officer or deputies, or any of its staff, shall be carried out by or against the SPCB on their behalf.[50] The SPCB is to be treated as a Crown body for the purposes of a number of important statutes, and given the privileges of such a body.[51]

---

[48]Section 21, and CSG Report, 3.2.51 *et seq.*
[49]See Rules 16.2–16.4.
[50]Section 40.
[51]The Scottish Parliamentary Corporate Body (Crown Status) Order 1999, SI 1999/677.

5. MAKING LAWS

INTRODUCTION

The Scottish Parliament has the power to make laws. As will have been seen from Chapter 2 above, the functions of government in which it is able to exercise that law-making power are wide. This chapter looks at the way in which proposals for legislation pass through the Parliament, taking into account also the mechanisms put in place by the Scotland Act and by the Parliament's Standing Orders to ensure that the Parliament does not make legislation in areas outside its field of responsibility.

The way in which the Parliament deals with legislation is similar in many respects to the way in which legislation is dealt with by the Westminster Parliament at present. In the Scottish Parliament, just as at Westminster, a proposal for legislation — a "Bill" — is normally to be considered both by committees and the full Parliament. At the end of the process, a legislative proposal must receive Royal Assent. When it has done so, it becomes law, termed an "Act of the Scottish Parliament."[1] In addition to legislation which passes through Parliament in that way, some subordinate legislation is made by Scottish Ministers.

However, there are also important differences between the two systems. There is no second chamber in the Scottish Parliament, unlike at Westminster. The Scottish Parliament and the Scottish Executive have some limited power to take part in the law-making procedure in areas which do not otherwise fall within its remit. And, perhaps most significantly, as the Parliament is restricted in its powers to make laws, the process whereby laws are made by it includes a number of features designed to ensure that the Parliament does not make laws in areas where it is not permitted to do so.

In this field, as in many others, the statutory requirements laid down in the Scotland Act were fleshed out in considerable detail by the CSG in its report, *Shaping Scotland's Parliament* and subsequently embodied the Parliament's Standing Orders.[2] In this chapter, the statutory provisions for Bills to pass through the Parliament are set out, and the procedures set out in Standing Orders are then looked at

---

[1] Section 28.

[2] The first Standing Orders for the Scottish Parliament were made by a statutory instrument of the UK Parliament: The Scotland Act 1998 (Transitory and Transitional Provisions) (Standing Orders and Parliamentary Publications) Order 1999 (SI 1999/1095). In December 1999, the Parliament resolved to adopt their own Standing Orders. These are largely based on the Standing Orders made by SI 1999/1095. The rules relating to the procedures for Bills are set out in Chapter 9 of the Standing Orders.

in some detail. Thereafter, the procedures for subordinate legislation are examined.

PRE-LEGISLATIVE SCRUTINY OF BILLS

Detailed provisions are built into the Scotland Act to ensure that each Bill proposed is subjected to scrutiny to prevent the creeping in of any provision which is outside the powers of the Scottish Parliament. This process of scrutiny begins even before a Bill is considered in detail by the Parliament. On or before the introduction of a Bill into the Parliament, the member of the Scottish Executive in charge of it must make a statement that the provisions of the Bill are within the legislative competence of the Parliament. The Presiding Officer must also consider the matter and make a statement to the Parliament as to whether or not the proposal is within that legislative competence.[3] Both presumably take legal advice before making such a statement.

Certain Law Officers — the Advocate General for Scotland, the Lord Advocate,[4] and the Attorney-General — also have a role in the scrutiny of Bills. If one of them has doubts as to whether any provision is within the legislative competence of the Parliament, he or she can refer the matter to the Judicial Committee of the Privy Council[5] for a decision. By contrast with the statement required before or at the time of the introduction of a Bill, this power to make a reference can only be exercised *after* a Bill has passed through the Parliament. Such a reference has to be made within four weeks of the Bill passing through the Parliament and during that period the Presiding Officer must not submit the Bill for Royal Assent. If the Judicial Committee decides that any provision of the Bill would not be within the legislative competence of the Parliament, the Presiding Officer is not permitted to submit it in its unamended form for the Royal Assent. Instead, the Bill returns to the Parliament to decide whether or not it wishes to reconsider the Bill.[6]

Since the UK joined the European Community, it has been possible for UK courts to refer certain questions relating to the interpretation of EC law to the European Court of Justice (ECJ) for a preliminary ruling. If a matter has been referred to the Judicial Committee of the Privy Council by one of the Law Officers, the Judicial Committee may make a further reference to the ECJ. Section 34 allows for the withdrawal of the reference if the Parliament decides that it wishes to reconsider the Bill.

Secretaries of State in the UK Government also have the power to intervene.[7] Any one of them may make an order prohibiting the Presiding Officer from submitting a Bill for Royal Assent in two sets of circumstances: first, where a Secretary of State believes that any

---

[3]Section 31.
[4]See Chapter 6 below.
[5]See Chapter 7 below.
[6]Sections 33 and 36.
[7]Section 35.

provision would be incompatible with any international obligations (other than obligations under European Community treaties, or arising from the European Convention on Human Rights), or the interests of defence or national security; and, second, where a Secretary of State believes that the Bill contains provisions which will modify the law as it relates to reserved powers *and* there are reasonable grounds to believe that the modification will have an adverse effect on that legal position. (As mentioned,[8] the Parliament does have a limited power to pass laws which affect matters reserved to the Westminster Parliament. The power given to a Secretary of State to prohibit legislation being submitted for Royal Assent allows the UK Government to stop the Scottish Parliament from passing such legislation.) Like the Law Officers, a Secretary of State has only four weeks after the passing of a Bill in which to decide whether to intervene and prohibit it from becoming law.

It should be noted that the power to make a reference can be exercised by *any* UK Secretary of State. It can be envisaged that it might be the Secretary of State with the relevant departmental interest who actually exercises the power (for example, in the first case, the Foreign Secretary); but no doubt political factors will also have a part to play in the decision as to which Secretary of State exercises the power. For example, the UK Government might consider it politically preferable for this supervisory power over the Scottish Parliament to be exercised by the Secretary of State for Scotland or any successor office.

If they wish, both the Law Officers and Secretaries of State can inform the Presiding Officer, at any time, that they do not intend to intervene to prevent a Bill becoming law. Unless the Bill is being reconsidered by the Parliament following an adverse decision by the Judicial Committee, they cannot then change their minds and intervene later to prevent the Bill receiving the Royal Assent.

THE STAGES OF BILLS

The processes of scrutiny described above take place either before or after a Bill makes its passage through the Parliament. In the UK Parliament, a Bill has to pass through a cumbersome process in both the House of Commons and the House of Lords before it can receive the Royal Assent and become an Act of Parliament. The stages in each house are:

- first reading;
- second reading;
- committee stage;
- report stage;
- third reading.

The pressures of time in the House of Commons are enormous. It is quite common for important clauses in Bills to receive little or no

---

[8]See Chapter 2 above.

scrutiny by MPs. The pace of business in the House of Lords is much more leisurely and their role in the legislative process is that of scrutiny and amendment so that any ambiguities and anomalies in a Bill may be removed.

The arrangements made for the passing of Bills in the Scottish Parliament are designed to simplify the process considerably compared with Westminster. The Scotland Act lays down[9] that a Bill should normally pass through the following stages in the Parliament:

- a general debate on a Bill with an opportunity for MSPs to vote on its general principles;
- consideration by MSPs of the details of the Bill (including an opportunity to vote on those details);
- a final stage at which a Bill can be passed or rejected.

However, the Parliament's Standing Orders allow for a particular Bill to modify some of these stages, so that an emergency measure can pass through the Parliament more quickly (although it is still subject to the scrutiny procedures described above).[10] In addition, in the case of Private Bills (see below) and certain Bills of primarily a formal nature, the Parliament may use a different procedure from that set out above.[11]

The Parliament's Standing Orders are also required by the Act to cater for the situation that would arise if the Judicial Committee has decided that a provision in a Bill goes beyond the legislative competence of the Parliament, or a Secretary of State has intervened to prevent the Bill being submitted for Royal Assent, as described above.[12] In either set of circumstances, the Parliament is required to reconsider the Bill in question. This reconsideration stage enables the MSPs to remove the offending provisions and bring the Bill within the legislative competence of the Parliament, or, as appropriate, deal with the concerns relating to international obligations or defence and national security. The Bill then has to go through the final stage again at which it can be approved or rejected.

The Scotland Act, therefore, only lays down the basic framework for the passage of Bills through the Parliament. The Parliament is given a great deal of freedom to regulate its own procedure in this respect, but here as in other areas, the CSG proposals offered a comprehensive model on which the Parliament's Standing Orders were based.

CONSULTATION

As the Parliament has no second House to act as a revising chamber, care has to be taken before a Bill starts on its progress to ensure that

---

[9] Section 36.
[10] Rule 9.21.
[11] Rule 9.17–9.20.
[12] Rule 9.9.

ambiguities and anomalies are removed as far as possible. Given that the legislative responsibilities of the Parliament, although significant, are more limited than those of Westminster, and that Bills are required to pass through a much more limited procedure than that which operates for UK Bills, the pressures on the timetable of the Scottish Parliament are less than those at Westminster. Bills can as matter of course pass through the Scottish Parliament within a matter of weeks of their introduction, and, as a result, the time in which any such ambiguities and anomalies in the Bill can be identified will be much shorter than is normally the case at Westminster (although the Parliament's Bills are of course subject to the scrutiny procedures described above which gives a second chance for any such difficulties to be picked up).

The CSG recognised this difficulty, and in its report it recommended that legislative proposals go through an extensive consultation procedure both before their introduction into Parliament and as they go through the legislative process. Such consultation serves the double purpose of providing an opportunity for such ambiguities and anomalies to be identified, and also to meet the political objective of ensuring maximum public involvement in the Parliament's work.[13]

The CSG emphasised that the consultation process should consist of more than an invitation to submit comments on specific legislative proposals. Accordingly, it recommended that legislative proposals from the Scottish Executive should have completed a consultative process before they are presented to the Parliament. It suggested that the Scottish Minister responsible for an area of policy should inform the relevant Committee of the Executive's intentions in its area of interest, and should discuss with it the relevant bodies to be involved in the consultation process. In order to ensure that the consultative procedure had been carried out, the Parliament's Standing Orders should require a Bill when introduced to the Parliament by the Executive to be accompanied by a memorandum giving details of the consultative process undertaken in that case. That would allow the committee concerned to arrange for further consultation if it felt that the Executive's consultation had been insufficient.

THE PASSAGE OF BILLS THROUGH THE PARLIAMENT

Executive Bills

As described above, the Scotland Act requires Bills normally to go through three stages. The Standing Orders of the Parliament which are based upon the recommendations of the CSG Report, lay down what is, in effect, a four stage process since Stage 1 is split into two parts. If a Bill is rejected at any of the stages, no further proceedings are to be taken on the Bill and a Bill in the same or similar terms may not be introduced within six months of the date on which it was

---

[13]CSG Report, 3.5.

rejected. A Bill falls if it has not been passed by the end of the session in which it was introduced, but a Bill in the same or similar terms may be introduced in the following session.[14]

A Bill is introduced by being lodged with the Clerk of the Parliament by the member in charge of the Bill. It must be in the proper form, be signed by the member introducing it and it may also be signed by other MSPs who support it.[15] On introduction, a Bill must be accompanied by a written statement by the Presiding Officer which indicates whether or not in his view the provisions of the Bill are within the legislative competence of the Parliament. If there are provisions which would be outwith the Parliament's legislative competence, he must indicate what these provisions are and give reasons for his view.[16] The Bill must also be accompanied by a Financial Memorandum which sets out the best estimates of costs to which the provisions of the Bill would give rise and the best estimates of the timescales over which these costs could be expected to arise. The Financial Memorandum must distinguish separately costs which could fall on the Scottish Administration, Scottish local authorities and other bodies, individuals and businesses.[17]

An Executive Bill, which is a Bill introduced by a member of the Scottish Executive, must also have several other accompanying documents. These are:

- a statement signed by the member of the Scottish Executive in charge of the Bill which states that in his or her view the provisions of the Bill would be within the legislative competence of the Parliament[18];
- explanatory notes which summarise objectively what each of the provisions of the Bill does and any other information necessary to explain the effect of the Bill;
- a policy memorandum which sets out—
  1. the policy objectives of the Bill;
  2. whether alternative ways of meeting those objectives were considered and, if so, why the approach in the Bill was adopted;
  3. the consultation, if any, which was undertaken on the Bill's objectives and the ways of meeting them and a summary of the outcome of the consultation;
  4. an assessment of the effects, if any, of the Bill on equal opportunities, human rights, island communities, local government, sustainable development and any other matter which the Scottish Ministers consider relevant.[19]

If the Bill contains any provision which charges expenditure on the

---

[14]A session of the Scottish Parliament is the four-year period from one general election to the next.

[15]Rule 9.2.

[16]Rule 9.3.1. This is part of the pre-legislative scrutiny of a Bill. See p 49 above.

[17]Rule 9.3.2.

[18]This is also part of the pre-legislative scrutiny of the Bill. See p 49 above.

[19]Rule 9.3.3.

Scottish Consolidated Fund there must also be an accompanying report signed by the Auditor General stating whether, in his view, the charge is appropriate.[20]

Once a Bill has been introduced and printed, it is referred by the Parliamentary Bureau[21] to the committee of the Parliament within whose remit the subject matter of the Bill falls. This committee is known as "the lead committee" and it is the task of the lead committee to consider and report on the general principles of the Bill. Where the subject matter of the Bill falls within the remit of more than one committee, one of these is designated as the lead committee, but the other committees may also consider the general principles of the Bill and report their views to the lead committee. If the Bill contains a provision which confers powers to make subordinate legislation, that provision must be referred to the Subordinate Legislation Committee which reports its views back to the lead committee.[22]

The introduction of a Bill is roughly equivalent to the First Reading stage of a Bill in the UK Parliament but much more is required of the member in charge of a Bill in the Scottish Parliament by way of accompanying documents, etc. than is required in the UK Parliament. The intention of these requirements is to improve the quality and the acceptability of Acts of the Scottish Parliament.

Stage 1

First, the lead committee considers the general principles of the Bill, taking account of the views, if any, of other committees, and it also considers the Scottish Executive's policy memorandum. It then prepares a report for the Parliament. Second, the full Parliament considers the general principles of the Bill in the light of the lead committee's report. (At this stage it is open to any MSP to move that the Bill be referred back to the lead committee for a further report. If that motion is agreed to, the Parliament's consideration of the Bill is postponed until the further report has been presented to it.) The Parliament then decides, on a vote if necessary, whether or not the Bill's general principles are agreed to. If they are, the Bill proceeds to Stage 2, if not, the Bill falls.[23] This stage is equivalent to the second reading stage in the UK Parliament.

Financial Resolution

Where a Bill contains provisions which introduce new expenditure or increase existing expenditure charged out of the Scottish Consolidated Fund or which impose or increase any tax or charge, there can be no proceedings after Stage 1 until the Parliament has, by

---

[20]Rule 9.3.4. For the Scottish Consolidated Fund and the Auditor General, see Chapter 8.
[21]For the Parliamentary Bureau, see Chapter 4.
[22]Rule 9.6.1, 9.6.2.
[23]Rule 9.6.3–9.6.7.

resolution, agreed to this. Such a resolution can only be moved by a member of the Scottish Executive or a junior Minister.[24]

Stage 2

The Bill is now referred back to the lead committee for detailed consideration. There must normally be a period of at least two weeks between the completion of Stage 1 and the beginning of Stage 2. The committee examines the Bill section by section[25] and considers amendments. Each section, whether amended or not, must be agreed to. It is open to any MSP to move an amendment to the Bill and participate in the debate on that amendment, but an MSP who is not a member of the committee may not vote on the amendment. It is possible for Stage 2 to be taken by a Committee of the Whole Parliament or by a committee which is not the lead committee.[26]

Stage 3

This stage is taken by the full Parliament and thus gives every MSP an opportunity to consider the Bill in its amended form. Normally two weeks must elapse between the completion of Stage 2 and the beginning of Stage 3 if the Bill has been amended at Stage 2. At Stage 3, the Parliament must decide whether the Bill is passed. It is open to any MSP to give notice of an amendment to be taken at this stage and it is possible for the member in charge of the Bill to move that no more than half the total number of sections should be referred back to the committee for further Stage 2 consideration but such a reference back may happen only once. If there is a vote on the question of whether the Bill is passed, the result is valid only if the number of members voting is more than a quarter of the total number of seats in the Parliament, i.e. a quarter of 129, which is presumably rounded up to 33. Stage 3 is the equivalent of the report and third reading stages in the UK Parliament.[27]

Subject to the possible four-weeks delay (referred to above[28]) and a reconsideration stage, the Bill is now ready to be presented to the Queen by the Presiding Officer for Royal Assent.

Reconsideration Stage

On occasion, it may be necessary for the Bill to be reconsidered by the Parliament. This will happen in the following circumstances:

- if one of the Law Officers has referred a question about the legislative competence to the Judicial Committee of the Privy Council; or

---

[24]Rule 9.12.

[25]Note that a Scottish Parliament Bill is divided into sections. A UK Parliament Bill is divided into clauses which become sections when the Bill becomes an Act of Parliament.

[26]Rule 9.7.

[27]Rule 9.8.

[28]See pp 49–50 above.

- if the Judicial Committee of the Privy Council has made a reference to the European Court of Justice for a preliminary ruling; and neither of these references has been decided; or
- if the Judicial Committee of the Privy Council has decided that the Bill or any provision of it is outwith the legislative competence of the Parliament; or
- if an order has been made by a Secretary of State prohibiting the Presiding Officer from presenting the Bill for Royal Assent.[29]

The reconsideration stage is taken by the full Parliament and the only amendments which may be moved at this stage are amendments to remove the offending sections of the Bill. Once the amendments have been disposed of, the Parliament decides the question of whether to approve the Bill.[30]

Table 2A, at the end of this chapter, shows how Executive Bills make their passage through the Parliament.

Committee Bills

Committee Bills are an innovation in the British law-making process and there is no equivalent procedure in the UK Parliament. The ability of committees of the Parliament to initiate legislation is in keeping with the spirit of giving them an opportunity to play a major part in the work of the Parliament. A proposal for a Committee Bill may be made either by a committee of the Parliament or by an individual MSP. If the proposal is made by an MSP, it is referred to the appropriate committee by the Parliamentary Bureau. (It also counts against the MSP's quota of two Member's Bills per session.) Prior to deciding whether to make a proposal, a committee may hold an inquiry into the need for the Bill. The proposal takes the form of a report to the Parliament setting out the committee's recommendations as to the provisions to be contained in the Bill, together with an explanation of the need for the Bill. If the Parliament agrees to the proposal, the convener of the committee introduces the Bill unless a member of the Scottish Executive or a junior Scottish Minister has indicated that an Executive Bill is to be introduced to give effect to the proposal. A Committee Bill must go through the three stages as for an Executive Bill, described above (with a reconsideration stage and a financial resolution if necessary), except that at Stage 1 it is referred immediately to the Parliament. A report by a lead committee on the Bill's general principles is not required as the committee initiating the Bill has already carried out all the preliminary work necessary.[31]

Table 2B at the end of this chapter shows how Committee Bills make their passage through Parliament.

---

[29]For more information, see pp 49–50 above.
[30]Rule 9.9.
[31]Rule 9.15.

Member's Bills

A Member's Bill is the equivalent of a Private Member's Bill in the UK Parliament. It is a Bill which is introduced by an MSP who is not a member of the Scottish Executive. Such members are sometimes referred to as backbenchers. Each member is entitled to introduce two Bills in any one session which gives a potential number of around 200 in each four-year session. There are two options open to an MSP for the introduction of a Member's Bill.

Option 1

The MSP submits to the Parliamentary Bureau a draft proposal for a Bill. The Parliamentary Bureau then refers the draft proposal to the relevant committee and the committee then decides whether to make the proposal as a Committee Bill.[32]

Option 2

The MSP gives notice of a proposal for a Bill, setting out the proposed short title of the Bill and a brief explanation of its purpose, by lodging it with the Clerk of the Parliament. The notice is then published in the Parliament's Business Bulletin for a period of one month. During that month the MSP must gather the support of at least eleven other MSPs. If sufficient support is not gathered during that period, the Bill falls and a similar proposal may not be introduced by any MSP within six months of the proposal falling.[33] A Member's Bill must pass through the three stages of a Bill described above, with a reconsideration stage and a financial resolution, if necessary.

Table 2B at the end of this chapter shows how a Member's Bill makes its way through the Parliament under Option 1 as a Committee Bill. For Option 2, see Table 2C.

Private Bills

A Private Bill is a Bill which is introduced by an individual person, by a body corporate or by an unincorporated association of persons. The person who introduces such a Bill is known as "the promoter". The promoter is seeking particular powers or benefits which go beyond or are in conflict with the general law. Thus, it is important that anyone who objects to the proposal has an opportunity to state his or her objections. A local authority, for example, may need additional powers to acquire land to construct a ring road or an airport or a harbour and may acquire these powers by promoting a Private Bill.[34] An individual may promote a Private Bill in relation to his or her estate, property, status or style. Such Bills promoted by individuals are likely to be fairly rare.

---

[32]Rule 9.15.4.
[33]Rule 9.14.
[34]It should be noted that all Bills which are not Private Bills are Public Bills.

A Private Bill can be introduced into the Parliament on 27th March or 27th November each year and it must be signed by or on behalf of the promoter. As with Executive Bills, it is referred to a lead committee for the first part of Stage 1. The committee prepares a report for the Parliament on the need for the Bill and the extent to which there is opposition to the Bill. To ascertain this, the committee may require the promoter to advertise the proposal, make various documents available for public inspection, give notice to any owners, occupiers and tenants of property affected by the proposal and invite objections to be lodged with the Clerk of the Parliament within a specified time. If the promoter fails to comply with any of the committee's requirements, the matter may be reported to the Parliament which may decide to reject the Bill.[35]

A Private Bill must go through the three stages for an Executive Bill (with a reconsideration stage, if necessary), but at Stage 2, the lead committee may arrange for an inquiry to be held to determine whether any of the Bill's proposals are necessary or to dispose of objections to the proposal.[36]

Emergency Bills

The process described above for Executive Bills has inbuilt delays of at least two weeks between Stages 1 and 2 and between Stages 2 and 3, if the Bill has been amended. There is also the possibility of a further four-weeks delay between the passing of a Bill and its submission for Royal Assent to allow for a reference by a Law Officer to the Judicial Committee of the Privy Council, a reference to the European Court of Justice or an intervention by a Secretary of State of the UK Parliament.[37] But there must be a procedure which allows the Scottish Executive to deal with emergencies. The Parliament's Standing Orders thus make special fast-track provisions for such situations.[38]

Any member of the Scottish Executive or a junior Scottish Minister may move that an Executive Bill shall be treated as an Emergency Bill. If the Parliament agrees, the Bill is referred immediately to the Parliament for Stage 1 consideration without the necessity of a report on the Bill's general principles from a committee. Stage 2 is taken by a Committee of the whole Parliament. The requirement of two weeks' delay between Stages 1 and 2 and 2 and 3 is dispensed with and all stages of the Bill are normally to be taken on the day that the Parliament decides that the Bill is to be treated as an Emergency Bill. The first Act passed by the Scottish Parliament, the Mental Health (Amendment) (Scotland) Act 1999, was treated as an Emergency Bill and passed through all stages and received the Royal Assent within a fortnight.

---

[35]Rule 9.17.
[36]Rule 9.17.6.
[37]See pp 49–50 above.
[38]Rule 9.21.

Budget Bills

A Budget Bill is an Executive Bill, the purpose of which is to authorise sums to be paid out of the Scottish Consolidated Fund or to authorise sums received to be applied without being paid into that fund.[39] A Budget Bill can only be introduced by a member of the Scottish Executive and does not need to be accompanied by a Financial Memorandum, Explanatory Notes or a Policy Memorandum.[40]

At Stage 1 a Budget Bill is referred immediately to the full Parliament for consideration of its principles and a decision as to whether these are agreed. A report from a committee on general principles is not required but Stage 2 of the Bill is taken by the Finance Committee. The requirement of a minimum of two-weeks delay between stages does not apply, but Stage 3 is not to begin earlier than 20 days after introduction of the Bill. Amendments to a Budget Bill may be moved only by a member of the Scottish Executive.[41]

If a Budget Bill is dependent on the Parliament passing a tax-varying resolution[42] and the Parliament rejects such a resolution, the Bill falls, but if a Bill falls or is rejected at any stage, a Bill in the same or similar terms can be introduced at any time thereafter.[43]

Miscellaneous other Bills

The Scottish Parliament may also pass:

- Consolidation Bills the purpose of which is to restate existing law with or without amendments, in accordance with recommendations of the Scottish Law Commission or the English Law Commission[44];
- Statute Law Repeal Bills the purpose of which is to repeal, in accordance with the Scottish Law Commission's recommendations, statute law which is out-of-date and no longer relevant[45];
- Statute Law Revision Bills the purpose of which is to revise statute law by repealing Acts which are no longer in force or have become unnecessary and re-enacting provisions of Acts of the Scottish Parliament or the UK Parliament which are otherwise spent.[46]

CHALLENGES TO THE LEGISLATION

As mentioned above, Acts passed by the Parliament are subject to various methods of pre-legislative scrutiny to ensure they do not

---

[39]For the Scottish Consolidated Fund, see pp 95–96 below.
[40]Rule 9.16.2.
[41]Rule 9.16.3–9.16.6.
[42]i.e. in accordance with section 73 of the Scotland Act. See pp 96–99 below.
[43]Rule 9.16.7–9.16.8.
[44]Rule 9.18.
[45]Rule 9.19. Such laws are known as "spent enactments".
[46]Rule 9.20.

stray beyond its legislative competence. However, the courts will have power even after legislation has been made to decide that the measure (or part of it) deals with matters outside the Parliament's legislative competence, and by so doing in effect strike down its legislation. As section 40(3) of the Act states that a court cannot make an order for suspension or reduction against the Parliament, it would appear that it could not as such "cancel" an item of legislation made by the Parliament. However, if asked to do so, the court would be able to declare that an item of legislation is outside the Parliament's legislative competence. Given that section 29(1) of the Scotland Act states that an Act of the Scottish Parliament that is outside its legislative competence is not law, the effect of such a declaration would be to make the item of legislation concerned null and void from the time that it was enacted. In practice, rather than leave it to the courts to make such a declaration, it is more likely that if an item of legislation were declared to be outside the Parliament's legislative competence, the Parliament would itself amend its legislation accordingly. If it did not, the UK Parliament or Ministers would be able to make the necessary amendment anyway.

Challenges to the Parliament's legislation are considered in more detail in Chapter 7 below.

SUBORDINATE LEGISLATION MADE BY SCOTTISH MINISTERS

Much UK legislation is enacted not as primary legislation which must pass through the full Parliamentary procedure, but as subordinate legislation in the form of either a statutory instrument or an Order in Council. Powers to make subordinate legislation are conferred on the Scottish Ministers and these powers can be exercised in any area in which the Scottish Parliament has legislative competence.[47] The Scotland Act places some restrictions on the power to make subordinate legislation. For example, serious criminal offences cannot be created by such legislation.[48] Once made, a piece of subordinate legislation is called a Scottish Statutory Instrument (SSI).

Procedures for making subordinate legislation

The Scotland Act does not lay down procedures for the making of subordinate legislation within devolved areas. Instead, the procedures are set out in the Parliament's Standing Orders.[49] The procedures are largely based on the Westminster model.

As at Westminster, most instruments are subject to either a negative procedure (subject to annulment) or an affirmative procedure (subject to approval). Under the negative procedure, the instrument becomes law unless there is a vote by the Parliament to annul the instrument.

---

[47]Scotland Act, ss 53, 54, 112.

[48]Scotland Act, s 113(10).

[49]The rules for making subordinate legislation are contained in Chapter 10 of the Parliament's Standing Orders.

Under the affirmative procedure, there must be a vote in favour of the instrument before it becomes law. The affirmative procedure is thus the stronger form of scrutiny. It is the parent Act which lays down which procedure is to be used and, in some cases, the parent Act may provide that the instrument is to be made without the approval of the Parliament.

Scrutiny by committees

The Scottish Parliament has a committee called the Subordinate Legislation Committee,[50] similar to the Joint Committee on Statutory Instruments at Westminster, which scrutinises the technical aspects of every piece of subordinate legislation which is laid before the Parliament. In the case of the Scottish Parliament, subordinate legislation is also scrutinised by at least one subject committee, a procedure which has no direct Westminster parallel.

An instrument (i.e. a proposed piece of subordinate legislation) is said to be laid before the Parliament if a copy of it is lodged with the Clerk of the Parliament during office hours. Once laid, the Clerk refers the instrument to the Subordinate Legislation Committee and to the lead committee, the subject committee within whose remit the subject matter of the instrument falls, unless the Parliament has decided that the instrument should be considered by the full Parliament. If the subject matter falls within the remit of more than one subject committee, one of the committees is designated as the lead committee and the instrument is sent to the other committee(s) which may make recommendations to the lead committee.[51]

The remit of the Subordinate Legislation Committee is to decide whether the attention of the Parliament should be drawn to the instrument on the following grounds:

- that it imposes a charge on the Scottish Consolidated Fund[52] or contains provisions requiring payments to be made to various bodies:
- that it is made under an Act (the parent Act) which specifically excludes challenge in the courts;
- that it appears to have retrospective effect although the parent Act does not confer the authority to do so;
- that there appears to be unjustifiable delay in publishing the instrument or in laying it before the Parliament;
- that there appears to be a doubt as to whether it is *intra vires*;
- that it raises a devolution issue;
- that it has been made by what appears to be an unusual or unexpected use of the powers conferred by the parent Act;

---

[50]The Subordinate Legislation Committee is one of the mandatory committees of the Scottish Parliament, i.e. the Parliament *must* establish such a committee. See Chapter 4.

[51]Rule 10.1, 10.2.

[52]For the Scottish Consolidated Fund, see Chapter 8.

- that for any special reason its form or meaning could be clearer;
- that its drafting appears to be defective;

or on any other ground which does not impinge on its substance or the policy behind it. The Subordinate Legislation Committee must report its decision with its reasons to the Parliament and to the lead committee within 20 days of the laying of the instrument.[53]

Motion for annulment (negative procedure)

The negative procedure is a weaker form of control of subordinate legislation because the instrument becomes law after a certain period if no MSP moves its annulment.

No later than 40 days after the instrument has been laid, any MSP (whether or not a member of the lead committee) can propose to the lead committee that nothing further should be done under the instrument. The lead committee is allowed to have a debate of no more than 90 minutes on this proposal and the MSP who has made that proposal, along with the Minister in charge of the instrument, may participate in the debate but not vote on the proposal.

The lead committee then reports to the Parliament, within 40 days of the instrument being laid, with its recommendations. If the lead committee recommends that no further action should be taken, i.e. that the instrument should not be made, a very limited debate takes place, a vote is taken if necessary and the instrument is then annulled.[54]

Motion for approval (affirmative procedure)

The affirmative procedure is a stronger form of control of subordinate legislation because the instrument cannot become law until it has been approved by the Parliament. The lead committee must decide whether to recommend to the Parliament that an instrument should be approved. Any member of the Scottish Executive or a junior Minister, even if not a member of the lead committee, may propose to the lead committee that it should recommend approval. As with the negative procedure, that member, and the Minister in charge of the instrument, may participate in the 90-minute debate but may not vote. The lead committee must make its recommendation to the Parliament within 40 days of its being laid. If approval is recommended, only very limited debate is allowed and, after a vote if necessary, the instrument is approved by the Parliament.[55]

Instruments which do not require the Parliament's approval

Some Acts of the Scottish Parliament may provide that an instrument laid before the Parliament may be made without the Parliament's

---

[53]Rule 10.3.
[54]Rule 10.4.
[55]Rule 10.6.

approval. Such instruments should not be contentious, but the Parliament's Standing Orders do allow MSPs to have some control over them. The procedure is very similar to the negative procedure described above. No later than 40 days after the instrument has been laid, any MSP may propose to the lead committee that the committee should recommend to the Parliament that the instrument be not made. That MSP and the Minister in charge of the instrument are entitled to participate in the 90-minute debate but may not vote if they are not members of the lead committee. If the lead committee recommends to the Parliament that the instrument should not be made, the procedure is as described above.[56]

Although the Scottish Ministers will normally be able to make subordinate legislation only in areas in which the Parliament has legislative competence, some possibilities exist for Scottish Ministers to make subordinate legislation in areas where the Parliament itself has not been given powers to legislate. The Act contains a power allowing for functions exercisable by a UK Minister to be transferred, by Order in Council, to Scottish Ministers (or to be exercised concurrently by both UK and Scottish Ministers), in so far as the functions concerned relate to Scotland.[57] This allows Scottish Ministers to make subordinate legislation in relation to matters concerning Scotland, but in which legislative power has not been devolved to the Parliament. (However, such a transfer can only take place with the approval of the Scottish Parliament, and also both Houses of the UK Parliament.[58]) The Act also includes specific provision allowing an Order in Council to be made giving powers to Scottish Ministers to make subordinate legislation concerning the regulation of the Tweed and Esk fisheries.[59]

THE LEGISLATIVE LOAD

At the beginning of the first session of the Parliament, the First Minister announced a legislative programme of eight Executive Bills. At the end of December 1999, when the Parliament had been in existence for six months, only one Act of the Scottish Parliament (asp) had reached the statute book, the Mental Health (Amendment) (Scotland) Act 1999, and that was an Emergency Bill. Three other Executive Bills and one Member's Bill were in progress while a further six Member's Bills were at the proposal stage. No Committee Bills had been introduced by that date. In contrast, the Parliament had made around 200 Scottish Statutory Instruments (SSIs) within the same period.

By the end of March 2000, there were two Acts of the Scottish Parliament on the statute book. Six Executive Bills and three

---

[56]Rule 10.5.
[57]Section 63. There is a parallel provision allowing for the transfer of functions from Scottish Ministers to UK Ministers in section 108.
[58]Schedule 7, para 2.
[59]Section 111.

Members' Bills were in progress with one Member's Bill at the proposal stage. Around 300 SSIs had been made.

UK SUBORDINATE LEGISLATION AND THE SCOTTISH PARLIAMENT AND MINISTERS

The Act also gives the Parliament and Scottish Ministers a degree of involvement in respect of other matters in which legislative competence has not been devolved to the Parliament.[60] The powers include those listed below, and can be grouped into three types.

Firstly, certain provisions allowing subordinate legislation to be made by Order in Council can only be exercised with the approval of the Parliament, as follows (in all but the first case the approval of both Houses of the UK Parliament is also required):

- the power to disqualify specified public office-holders from becoming an MSP[61];
- the power to modify the list of reserved matters on which the Parliament cannot legislate[62];
- the power to transfer additional functions from UK Ministers to Scottish Ministers[63];
- the power to make payment to opposition political parties to assist MSPs in carrying out their duties[64];
- for functions exercisable by Scottish Ministers to be transferred in whole or in part to UK Ministers.[65]

Secondly, there are certain matters in respect of which the Scottish Parliament can annul proposals for UK subordinate legislation, as follows:

- the transfer of property and liabilities from UK Ministers to Scottish Ministers or the Lord Advocate (and vice versa)[66];
- specifying functions which a UK Minister can arrange by agreement to be carried out by a Scottish Minister or the Lord Advocate (and vice versa)[67];
- an order made by the Scottish Minister setting the level of the deposit (caution) which has to be lodged by a person seeking the disqualification of an MSP[68];
- the adaptation of the functions of a "cross-border public authority"[69] and the transfer of the property and liabilities of such bodies (unless, in these cases, the Parliament (and the UK

---

[60]Schedule 7.
[61]Section 15.
[62]Section 30.
[63]Section 63.
[64]Section 97.
[65]Section 108.
[66]Section 109.
[67]Section 93.
[68]Section 18.
[69]See Chapter 9 below on cross-border public authorities.

Parliament) has previously approved the subordinate legislation in question).[70]

(If the UK subordinate legislation in the above cases, except in the case of setting the level of caution, changes the text of an Act of Parliament, the Scottish Parliament, and both Houses of the UK Parliament, have to approve the proposal by a positive vote in support of it).

Thirdly, there are certain cases in which the Scottish Ministers have to be consulted before subordinate legislation is made by the relevant UK authority, including the following:

- an order made by the UK Treasury designating those government receipts which are to be payable into the Scottish Consolidated Fund — the Treasury is required to consult with the Scottish Ministers before making such designation[71];
- the exercise of certain powers by UK Ministers over cross-border public authorities — in some circumstances the UK Minister must consult the Scottish Ministers before exercising functions in relation to a cross-border public authority[72];
- subordinate legislation transferring certain functions to Scottish Ministers where that modifies certain obligations under international or EU law — the Scottish Ministers must be consulted before any such legislation is made.[73]

---

[70]Sections 89 and 90.
[71]Section 64.
[72]Section 88; and see Chapter 9 below.
[73]Section 106.

The legislative process of the Scottish Parliament

TABLE 2A

Executive Bills

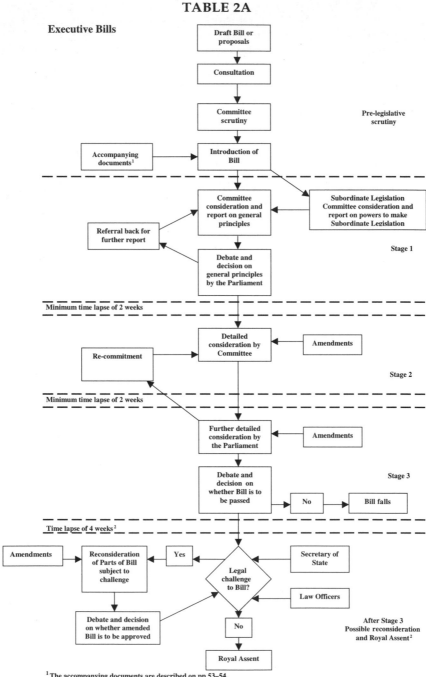

[1] The accompanying documents are described on pp 53–54.
[2] N.B. Royal Assent can take place after less than 4 weeks if the Secretary of State and Law Officers waive their right to challenge.

TABLE 2B

Committee Bills

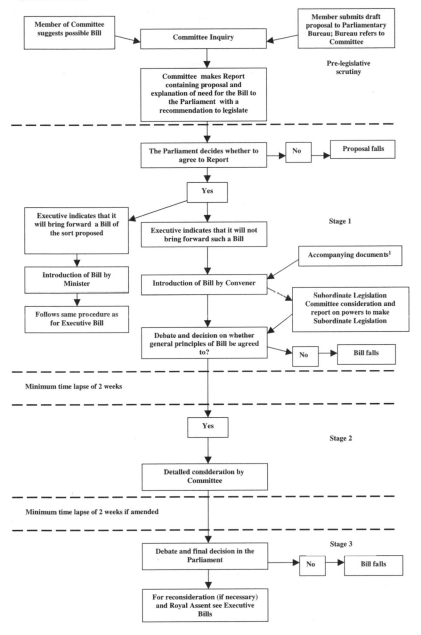

| Member of Committee suggests possible Bill | → | Committee Inquiry | ← | Member submits draft proposal to Parliamentary Bureau; Bureau refers to Committee |

Pre-legislative scrutiny

Committee makes Report containing proposal and explanation of need for the Bill to the Parliament with a recommendation to legislate

The Parliament decides whether to agree to Report → No → Proposal falls

Yes

Stage 1

Executive indicates that it will bring forward a Bill of the sort proposed

Executive indicates that it will not bring forward such a Bill

Accompanying documents[1]

Introduction of Bill by Minister

Introduction of Bill by Convener

Subordinate Legislation Committee consideration and report on powers to make Subordinate Legislation

Follows same procedure as for Executive Bill

Debate and decision on whether general principles of Bill be agreed to? → No → Bill falls

Minimum time lapse of 2 weeks

Yes

Stage 2

Detailed consideration by Committee

Minimum time lapse of 2 weeks if amended

Stage 3

Debate and final decision in the Parliament → No → Bill falls

For reconsideration (if necessary) and Royal Assent see Executive Bills

[1]The accompanying documents are described on pp 53–54.

TABLE 2C

Members' Bills

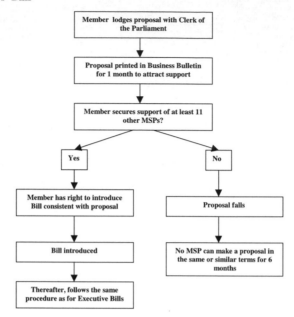

6. THE SCOTTISH GOVERNMENT

INTRODUCTION

The establishment of a Scottish Parliament has given Scotland not only a legislature, but also a Government which may take executive action over the whole range of devolved functions. The Scotland Act describes it as the Scottish Administration. It is based on the Westminster model of parliamentary government. The Ministers are drawn from the ranks of the MSPs and are accountable to them. In the UK government the rules relating to the appointment of the Prime Minister and the other Ministers of the UK Parliament are largely unwritten and are based on convention. The equivalent rules for the appointment of the First Minister and the other Ministers of the Scottish Parliament are statutory and are to be found in Part II of the Scotland Act 1998.

The Scottish Executive consists of the First Minister, Scottish Ministers and the Scottish Law Officers, the Lord Advocate and the Solicitor General for Scotland.[1] No person who holds Ministerial office in the UK Government is allowed to be appointed as a minister in the Scottish Administration. Thus, anyone who is elected to the Scottish Parliament and who already holds Ministerial office in Her Majesty's Government in any of the UK Departments of State has to give that office up if he or she is to become a Scottish Minister. This rule applies also to the First Minister. Thus, Donald Dewar, who was Secretary of State for Scotland prior to the first general election to the Scottish Parliament in 1999, resigned from that office in order to be appointed as a member of the Scotish Executive and First Minister.

THE FIRST MINISTER

The First Minister is the equivalent of the Prime Minister. The First Minister is appointed by the Queen from among the Members of the Scottish Parliament within 28 days of a general election and holds office "at Her Majesty's pleasure".[2] Theoretically this means that the First Minister could be dismissed by the Queen for good reason or for none. In practice, the First Minister holds office as long as he or she can command the support of the majority of the MSPs. Therefore, the person appointed as First Minister is normally the leader of the party able to command the majority support of the MSPs. Given the electoral system to the Scottish Parliament which has an element of

---

[1]Section 44.
[2]Section 45(1).

proportional representation in it, it is unlikely that any one single party will win a clear majority of the seats. In the first elections the Labour Party won 56 of the 129 seats and thus did not have a clear majority. A coalition agreement was reached with the Liberal Democrats[3] and as part of the agreement, the leader of the Labour Party, Donald Dewar, emerged as the favoured candidate for the post of First Minister with the Leader of the Liberal Democrats, Jim Wallace, as his deputy.

The Parliament's Standing Orders set out the procedure for the nomination of an MSP for appointment as First Minister.[4] Any member may nominate a candidate by submitting a nomination to the Clerk of the Parliament in writing. To be valid, the nomination must be seconded by another MSP. The candidates must have taken the oath of allegiance before voting takes place. An electronic voting system is normally used, but if the Presiding Officer thinks that that system cannot be used for any reason or that it has produced an unreliable result, the vote may be taken by ballot or by roll call or any other method. The names of the candidates are read out by the Presiding Officer and then there is a vote or a series of votes until one single candidate emerges who has the support of the majority of MSPs voting.[5] The quorum for this vote is 25 per cent plus one which seems very low for such an important decision. Following the selection of the candidate by the Parliament, the Presiding Officer recommends that candidate to the Queen for appointment and the Queen appoints the candidate.

If the office of First Minister is vacant, or he or she is for any reason, such as prolonged illness, unable to act, his or her functions are exercisable by another MSP designated by the Presiding Officer.[6] No doubt the Presiding Officer would consult the party leaders privately to try to identify a Member who would be generally acceptable. When the First Minister, Donald Dewar, became ill in 2000, the Deputy First Minister, Jim Wallace, deputised. The First Minister may resign at any time and must do so if the Scottish Executive loses the confidence of the Scottish Parliament.[7]

THE FUNCTIONS OF THE FIRST MINISTER

The First Minister is, in many ways, the Scottish Prime Minister. He or she is normally the leader of the party with the largest number of seats in the Scottish Parliament, the Leader of the Scottish Executive

---

[3]The terms of the coalition agreement are to be found in *Partnership for Scotland: An Agreement for the First Scottish Parliament* (May 1999).

[4]The rules relating to the nomination of the First Minister and the appointment of members of the Scottish Executive are contained in Chapter 4 of the Parliament's Standing Orders.

[5]The procedures relating to the selection of the First Minister are to be found in Rule 11.10 of the Parliament's Standing Orders.

[6]Section 45(4).

[7]Section 45(2).

and the chief channel of communication with the UK Prime Minister.

Certain powers of appointment are specifically conferred on the First Minister by the Scotland Act which, in the case of the UK Prime Minister, are largely conventional. The First Minister, with the agreement of the Parliament, recommends Ministers, junior Ministers and the Law Officers to the Queen for appointment. Ministers and junior Ministers may be removed from office by the First Minister. In the case of the Law Officers, the First Minister may, with the agreement of the Parliament, recommend their removal to the Queen.[8] The Act allows for executive functions to be conferred on the First Minister alone and the doctrine of collective responsibility does not apply to his or her acts or omissions.[9]

The crucial difference between the Scottish First Minister and the UK Prime Minster is that the former will almost always be the head of a coalition government, whereas the UK Prime Minister will normally have a working majority – at least as long as the first past the post system of voting is retained for elections to Westminster. Coalition with another political grouping inevitably constrains the freedom of action of the First Minister. In the allocation of portfolios to Ministers, he or she has to negotiate with the Leader of the smaller party or parties in the coalition as to how many Ministerial posts each party will have. The Labour/Liberal Democrat coalition which emerged after the first elections in May 1999 allocated two Ministerial posts and two junior Ministerial posts to the Liberal Democrats. The UK Prime Minister does not normally have this constraint. The same process of inter-party negotiation applies in the policies to be adopted, the prioritisation of Bills, the convenership of committees and many other aspects of the business of government.[10]

Nevertheless, the office of First Minister is a very powerful one. By presiding at Cabinet meetings, and setting its agenda to a large extent, the First Minister can control discussion and the process of decision-making. He or she is expected to make major policy statements and intervene in the pressing issues of the day, such as Scottish industrial closures. The press and other media see the First Minister as Scotland's Prime Minister and give him or her enormous public exposure.

The appointment and removal of judges

The appointment and removal of judges is also largely within the First Minister's powers.[11] The two most senior judges in Scotland are the Lord President of the Court of Session and the Lord Justice Clerk. The Prime Minister recommends the names of appropriate persons to the Queen, but he cannot recommend anyone for appointment who

---

[8]Sections 47–49.
[9]Section 52(5)(a).
[10]See *Partnership for Scotland: An Agreement for the First Scottish Parliament* (May 1999).
[11]Section 95.

has not first been nominated by the First Minister. The First Minister also recommends to the Queen the names of persons for appointment as the other judges of the Court of Session, sheriffs principal and sheriffs, but only after consultation with the Lord President.

In practice it is the Lord Advocate[12] who selects candidates for appointment as judges and sheriffs and recommends them to the First Minister. In February 2000, amidst some controversy, the first Lord Advocate in the new Scottish Parliament, Lord Hardie, recommended himself to the First Minister for appointment as a Court of Session judge. He was duly appointed and the Solicitor-General, Colin Boyd, was promoted to fill the vacancy.

Giving the power of appointment of judges to the First Minister, who is a party politician, on the recommendation of the Lord Advocate who is also a member of the Scottish Executive has been criticised as undermining the independence of the judiciary and has in fact led to the decision to suspend temporary sheriffs.[13] However, the Scotland Act contains provisions which would enable the Parliament to establish a judicial appointments committee which the First Minister would have to consult before making recommendations as to the appointment of judges and sheriffs.[14] The use of such a committee might be seen as distancing the First Minister and the Lord Advocate, to some extent, from the accusation of making political appointments. It has also been suggested that the Parliament or one of its committees should have a role in the vetting of candidates for judicial appointments.

The Scottish Executive issued a consultation paper on the possibility of a judicial appointments commission in the spring of 2000.[15]

The power to remove a judge of the Court of Session is even more controversial and provoked a great deal of debate during the passage of the Scotland Act through the House of Lords. Prior to the establishment of the Scottish Parliament, there was no power to remove such a judge from office in Scotland. The position in England is different where a judge may be removed from office following an address from the House of Commons and the House of Lords to the Queen. The Scotland Bill as originally drafted would have allowed the First Minister to recommend to the Queen the removal of a Court of Session judge following a resolution of the Parliament which was supported by at least two-thirds of the total number of MSPs.

The provisions in the Scotland Act now build in a further stage to protect the independence of the judges. The procedure is to be governed by an Act of the Scottish Parliament. If there is any question of a judge of the Court of Session or the Chairman of the Scottish Land Court being unfit for office through inability, neglect of duty or misbehaviour, the First Minister may set up a tribunal of at least three persons, chaired by a member of the Judicial Committee of the Privy

[12]For more information on the Lord Advocate, see p 74 below.
[13]Starrs & Chalmers v Ruxton 2000 SLT 42, and Chapter 10, n 14.
[14]Scotland Act 1998, s 95(5).
[15]Judicial Appointments: An Inclusive Approach.

Council, to investigate and report on the matter. The First Minister must set up such a tribunal if requested to do so by the Lord President of the Court of Session and may do so in other circumstances if it is considered to be necessary. If the tribunal reports, in writing and with reasons, that the judge is unfit for office for one of the reasons given above, the First Minister is to move a resolution before the Parliament that a recommendation should be made to the Queen that the judge should be removed from office. The First Minister must obtain the approval of the Parliament, but there is now no requirement of a special majority. If the judge to be removed from office is either the Lord President or the Lord Justice Clerk, the First Minister must consult the Prime Minister. The lesser penalty of suspension may be imposed, if the Act of the Scottish Parliament includes this as a possibility.

SCOTTISH MINISTERS

The First Minister appoints a team of Scottish Ministers. Each Minister must be a Member of the Scottish Parliament. Ministers are appointed with the Queen's approval, but the First Minister must first seek the agreement of the Parliament to the nominations before submitting names to the Queen.[16] This is different from the procedure at Westminster where the Prime Minister can recommend to the Queen the appointment of whomsoever he wishes to Ministerial office, subject of course to political considerations, without having to secure the agreement of Parliament. Standing Orders allow the First Minister to seek Parliament's approval for the appointment of Scottish Ministers either individually or *en bloc*. The Parliament is able to reject, but not to substitute the names of particular individuals in the First Minister's list. A simple majority of those voting is sufficient to secure Parliament's agreement and again the quorum is 25 per cent plus one.[17] The allocation of portfolios to Ministers is a decision for the First Minister alone subject to negotiation with the coalition partner(s), if any, and is not included in the motion seeking the Parliament's approval to appointment.

Scottish Ministers, like the First Minister, hold office at Her Majesty's pleasure. They may be removed from office by the First Minister and must resign if they lose the confidence of the Parliament.[18] The Presiding Officer notifies the Parliament of any resignation made by a member of the Scottish Executive. Ministers cease to hold office if they cease to be MSPs for any reason (other than the calling of an election) such as bankruptcy or insanity.

In the UK Parliament, whose members are elected under the first past the post system, it is usual for one party to have an outright majority. Thus, UK ministers are normally MPs from one single

---

[16]Section 47(2).
[17]The procedures relating to the appointment of Scottish Ministers are found in Rule 4.6 of the Parliament's Standing Orders.
[18]Section 47(3).

political party, the party of government. In the Scottish Parliament some of whose members are elected under the regional list system discussed above,[19] coalition government will be the norm and Scottish Ministers are appointed from the MSPs of the parties forming the coalition. The number of Ministers in the UK Cabinet is around 22. The number of Scottish Ministers appointed to the first Scottish Executive is 10.

In addition to the oath of allegiance to the Queen which all members of the Scottish Parliament must take on election, members of the Scottish Executive must take the official oath as laid down in the Promissory Oaths Act 1868, in the following terms: ''I do swear that I will well and truly serve Her Majesty Queen Elizabeth in the office of Scottish Minister''.

THE SCOTTISH LAW OFFICERS

There are two Scottish Law Officers, namely, the Lord Advocate and his or her deputy, the Solicitor General, who act as the senior legal advisers to the Scottish Executive and are themselves members of the Scottish Executive. In other words, they are political appointments. The Lord Advocate is also the head of the systems of criminal prosecution and investigation of deaths in Scotland and must act independently in those capacities.

Unlike the rest of the Scottish Ministers, they do not have to be Members of the Scottish Parliament and neither the first two Lords Advocate nor the first two Solicitors-General were elected members of the Scottish Parliament. It is quite possible that they may not even be members of a political party (which is unlikely to be the case with any of the Scottish MSPs). The reason for this is that they have to be legally qualified and it may not be possible to find two MSPs who have the appropriate qualifications. They do, however, have to have the approval of Parliament before they can be appointed[20] and the same procedure as that used for the appointment of Scottish Ministers is used for securing the agreement of Parliament.[21] If they are not Members of the Parliament, they can still participate in Parliamentary proceedings but they may not vote.[22] They are able to participate in debates and answer questions, attend sessions of Committees, and steer through Parliament any Bills or secondary legislation for which they have responsibility. However, if asked any question in Parliament or asked to produce any document by the Parliament which relates to the operation of the system of criminal prosecution in a

---

[19]See Chapter 3 above.

[20]Section 48.

[21]The procedures relating to the appointment, removal and parliamentary participation of the Law Officers are contained in rules 4.3–4.5 of the Parliament's Standing Orders.

[22]Section 27.

particular case, they may decline to do so on the grounds that it might prejudice criminal proceedings in that case or would otherwise be contrary to the public interest.

The First Minister, having obtained the agreement of the Parliament to their nominations, recommends their appointment to the Queen. They may resign at any time and must do so if the Scottish Executive loses the confidence of the Parliament. However, if the Lord Advocate has to resign as a result of a vote of no confidence in the Scottish Executive, he is deemed to remain in office as head of the systems of criminal prosecution and investigation of deaths in Scotland until a successor is appointed.[23]

This is one of a number of provisions in the Scotland Act designed to safeguard the independence of the Scottish Law Officers. In addition, it is outwith the legislative competence of the Scottish Parliament to attempt to pass an Act which contains a provision which would remove the Lord Advocate from his position as head of the systems of criminal prosecution and investigation of deaths in Scotland.[24] Any decisions taken by him in either of those capacities must be taken by him independently.

However, the Lord Advocate is a member of the Scottish Executive and thus has a seat in the Scottish Cabinet. This has come in for a certain amount of criticism from one of Scotland's most senior judges, Lord McCluskey, who argues that the Lord Advocate's membership of the Executive undermines his judicial independence.[25]

JUNIOR SCOTTISH MINISTERS

The First Minister may also appoint junior Scottish Ministers. They are not technically members of the Scottish Executive as defined in section 44 although they are considered as such. Section 49 of the Scotland Act which deals with their appointment does not set any limit to their number. In the UK Government there is a statutory limit. Not more than 95 members of the House of Commons may hold Ministerial office. The purpose of this (in theory at least) is to prevent the Executive from dominating Parliament. Political considerations and public opinion no doubt work together to ensure that a reasonable limit is set in the Scottish Parliament and in the first Parliament the number of junior Ministers appointed was 10. Junior Scottish Ministers are appointed in the same way as Scottish Ministers. With the agreement of the Parliament, the First Minister recommends their appointment to the Queen. They, too, hold office at Her Majesty's pleasure, may be removed from office by the First Minister, may resign at any time, and must do so if the Scottish Executive loses the confidence of the Scottish Parliament.

---

[23]Section 48(3).
[24]Section 29(2)(e).
[25]See *The Herald*, 27th December 1999.

MOTIONS OF NO CONFIDENCE

It is a convention of the UK constitution that the Prime Minister and his Ministers resign if they lose a motion of no confidence. The Scotland Act puts this into statutory form. Sections 45(2), 47(3)(c), 48(2) and 49(4)(c) require the resignation of the First Minister, the Scottish Ministers, the Law Officers and junior Ministers respectively if Parliament resolves that the Scottish Executive no longer enjoys the confidence of the Parliament. If the Parliament subsequently fails to nominate a successor as First Minister, a general election has to be called.

Any MSP is able to move a motion of no confidence in the Scottish Executive. The motion must be supported by at least 25 other MSPs to be included in the business programme of the Parliament. Normally, at least two days' notice of a motion of no confidence should be given, but the Parliamentary Bureau may decide that a shorter period is appropriate.[26] Such a motion requires a simple majority of those voting (subject to a quorum) for approval. The Parliament is also able to consider a motion of no confidence in a named Minister. This would not automatically lead to the resignation of the Minister as the Scotland Act does not require this. However, the position of that Minister might become untenable after losing the confidence of the Parliament and the First Minister might ask the Minister to resign.

THE CIVIL SERVICE

The Scottish Ministers may appoint such staff as they consider appropriate. These staff are in the Home Civil Service, as are staff serving in other departments of the Scottish Executive, including the Lord Advocate's Department.[27] The holders of various offices such as the Registrar General of Births, Deaths and Marriages for Scotland and the Keepers of the Records and Registers of Scotland are also in the Home Civil Service as are their staff. The UK Government considers that maintaining a unified Home Civil Service is essential for the preservation of the Union. It also preserves a career structure in the UK for Civil Servants and ensures that their terms and conditions of service are appropriately protected. Responsibility for the management of that staff ultimately remains with the Minister for the Civil Service (*i.e.* the Prime Minister), but in practice responsibility for the day to day management of staff is delegated to the Scottish Ministers as happens for UK Government departments.

The officers in the Scottish Executive are divided into six major departments. These are:

- The Scottish Executive Development Department which has responsibility for local government, social inclusion, housing,

---

[26]The procedures relating to motions of no confidence are found in Rule 8.12 of the Parliament's Standing Orders.
[27]Section 51.

transport, planning, building control and European Structural Funds;

- The Scottish Executive Education Department which has responsibility for primary and secondary education and for the arts, cultural and built heritage and architectural policy, sport and Gaelic;
- The Scottish Executive Health Department which has responsibility for all aspects of the NHS in Scotland;
- The Scottish Executive Enterprise and Lifelong Learning Department which has responsibility for business and industry, further and higher education and lifelong learning;
- The Scottish Executive Justice Department which has responsibility for the police and fire services, Scottish courts administration, criminal justice social work, legal aid and electoral procedures; and
- The Scottish Executive Rural Affairs Department which has responsibility for agriculture, the environment and fisheries.

There are also the Executive Secretariat, Corporate Services and Finance Sections.

MINISTERIAL FUNCTIONS

Ministers of the UK Government exercise various powers most of which are conferred on them by an Act of Parliament. A few derive from the common law and are called prerogative powers. As the Scottish Parliament began to pass its own Acts, powers were conferred by these Acts on Scottish Ministers. However, the Scotland Act contains a section which transferred existing prerogative and executive functions relating to devolved matters virtually in their entirety from UK Ministers to Scottish Ministers.[28] This was a sensible provision for the early days of the Scottish Parliament. Many of the early decisions taken by the Scottish Executive derived from powers conferred by an Act of the UK Parliament on a Secretary of State, usually the Secretary of State for Scotland. This section enabled the Scottish Ministers to take over immediately without requiring any other piece of empowering legislation.

As the Scottish Parliament started to enact its own legislation, section 52 enabled functions to be conferred directly on the First Minister, the Lord Advocate and the Scottish Ministers by Acts of the Scottish Parliament or subordinate legislation. In the UK Parliament the duties of Secretaries of State are, in theory, interchangeable and this theory is continued into the Scottish Parliament with the provision that statutory functions may be exercised by any member of the Scottish Executive. The acts and omissions of any of them (other than the specific functions conferred on the First Minister or the Lord Advocate) are to be treated as the acts and omissions of each of them. This puts into statutory form the doctrine of collective responsibility.

---

[28]Section 53.

There are some exceptions to the general rule about the transfer of powers from the UK Ministers to the Scottish Ministers where it makes sense for a UK Minister to share powers with Scottish Ministers, for example, the provision of grants or loans for transport infrastructure, the promotion of exports and the funding of scientific research.[29] UK Ministers also retain the power to make regulations for Scotland in order to implement European Community obligations and Scottish Ministers have no power to make subordinate legislation or to do any act which is incompatible with European Community law or with rights under the European Convention on Human Rights.[30]

COLLECTIVE RESPONSIBILITY

The acceptance of the constitutional doctrine of collective responsibility forms part of the coalition agreement between the Labour Party and the Liberal Democrats.[31] The partners in the coalition accept that all the business of the Scottish Executive, including decisions, announcements, expenditure plans, proposed legislation and appointments, should be supported collectively by all members of the Executive and that there should be an appropriate level of consultation and discussion to ensure the support of all Ministers. Ministers have the opportunity to express their views frankly as decisions are reached, and opinions expressed and advice given within the Executive remain private. However, once a decision is reached, it is to be binding on all Ministers. Any Minister who cannot accept a decision of the Executive is expected to resign.

In addition to the doctrine of collective responsibility, there is a code of guidance on procedures for members of the Scottish Executive and junior Scottish Ministers.[32]

EXECUTIVE DEVOLUTION IN RELATION TO RESERVED MATTERS

The White Paper made it clear that the Scottish Executive was to be responsible for the exercise of certain administrative functions in areas where the law-making powers are reserved to the UK Government.[33] This is termed executive devolution. Prior to devolution, most of these functions were performed by the Secretary of State for Scotland. These include:

- the administration in Scotland of European Structural Funds;
- civil nuclear emergency planning;

---

[29]Section 56.
[30]Section 57.
[31]*Partnership for Scotland: An Agreement for the First Scottish Parliament* (May 1999), para 2.6.
[32]Ibid, Part III.
[33]The Scottish Ministerial Code, Scottish Executive (August 1999).

- powers and duties in relation to electricity supply;
- administration of firearms licensing;
- establishment and operation of certain public sector pension schemes;
- enforcing medicine legislation;
- designation of casino areas;
- various powers and duties relating to transport.

In most cases these are now transferred to Scottish Ministers for them to exercise instead of UK Ministers. Some are exercisable concurrently by Scottish Ministers and UK Ministers, while others are exercised by a UK Minister, but only after consultation with, or with the consent of, the Scottish Ministers.

The First Scottish Cabinet

(Appointed 1999)

First Minister
Donald Dewar
(Labour)

Deputy First Minister
Jim Wallace
(Liberal Democrat)

The Scottish Ministers

Wendy Alexander	Sarah Boyack	Susan Deacon	Ross Finnie	Sam Galbraith	Tom McCabe	Jack McConnell	Henry McLeish
(Labour)	(Labour)	(Labour)	(Lib. Dem)	(Labour)	(Labour)	(Labour)	(Labour)

(The Law Officers are members of the Scottish Executive: Andrew Hardie: Lord Advocate — resigned Feb 2000, Colin Boyd: Solicitor General — promoted to Lord Advocate Feb 2000)

Junior Scottish Ministers

Jackie Baillie	Rhona Brankin	Iain Gray	John Home Robertson	Frank McAveety	Angus McKay	Alisdair Morrison	Peter Peacock	Ian Smith	Nicol Stephen
(Labour)	(Labour)	(Labour)	(Labour)	(Labour)	(Labour)	(Labour)	(Labour)	(Lib. Dem)	(Lib. Dem)

Scottish Executive — Overview

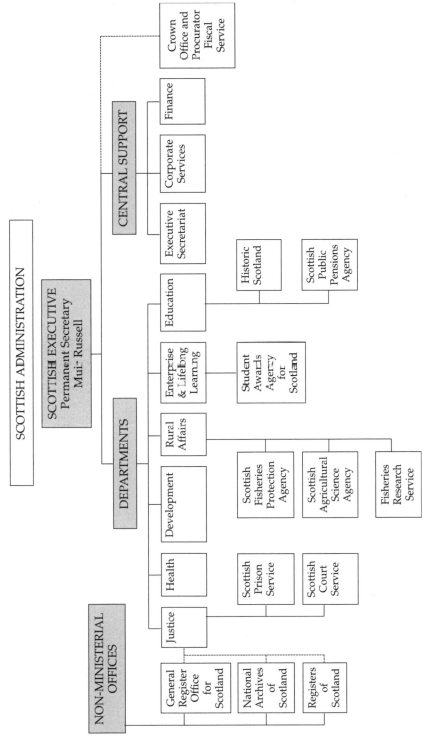

7. RELATIONS WITH WESTMINSTER AND THE RESOLUTION OF DISPUTES

INTRODUCTION

As explained in Chapter 2, the Scottish Parliament has its powers devolved to it by the UK Parliament and the UK Parliament has not relinquished its sovereignty. The Scottish Parliament is, therefore, a body subordinate to the UK Parliament and could be abolished by it. However, as long as the Scottish Parliament remains popular as an institution with the Scottish people, the UK Parliament is unlikely to take such drastic action. Nevertheless, the UK Parliament retains some important controls over the Scottish Parliament.

LEGISLATIVE AND EXECUTIVE CONTROLS

As has been explained in Chapter 2, two areas reserved to the UK Parliament by Schedule 5 to the Scotland Act are the Union of the Kingdoms of Scotland and England and the Parliament of the UK and most of the provisions of the Scotland Act are protected from modification by Schedule 4. A Scottish Executive led by the SNP, therefore, would not be able to pass a valid Act of the Scottish Parliament declaring Scottish independence.

In addition, section 28 of the Scotland Act 1998, which deals with the legislative powers of the Scottish Parliament, contains a subsection which states quite unequivocally that section 28 does not affect the power of the UK Parliament to make laws for Scotland.[1] It is likely that Westminster will rarely, if ever, use this power to pass Acts in areas which lie wholly within the devolved competence of the Scottish Parliament. However, from time to time issues will undoubtedly arise where UK legislation in matters reserved to Westminster will require consequential changes in Scottish legislation if they are to be fully operative in Scotland. An early example of such a measure was the Immigration and Asylum Act 1999, which became law in November 1999. This Act was concerned with matters which are undoubtedly reserved to the Westminster Parliament, but included a number of provisions in areas which are normally devolved to the Scottish Parliament (e.g. in housing, education, and social work). The White Paper *Scotland's Parliament* also envisaged that there might be instances (such as might arise, for example, in questions relating to international obligations where they touched upon both devolved and reserved matters) where it would be more convenient for

---

[1]Section 28(7).

legislation to be passed by the UK Parliament. An early example of such legislation was the Food Standards Act 1999, which established a Food Standards Agency. The legislation passed through the UK Parliament after the Scottish Parliament had acquired its full powers, and food safety is a matter which is devolved to the Scottish Parliament. However, the UK and Scottish governments decided that it would be appropriate for the legislation to be introduced on a UK-wide basis, if the Scottish Parliament consented, as it duly did. It should be noted that the Food Standards Act does have a separate Scottish executive machinery and advisory committee, and will report to both the Scottish and UK Parliaments. Moreover, it is made clear in the Act that it does not detract from the Scottish Parliament's right to legislate in the area of food safety if it so wishes.[2]

It was also envisaged in the White Paper, *Scotland's Parliament*, that the early establishment of liaison machinery (as discussed later in this chapter) would ensure that most potential disputes about the respective powers of the two Parliaments were resolved "quickly and amicably".[3] The prospect of clashes may, of course, arise more frequently if the Scottish Parliament is under the control of a political party or coalition led by a party which is different from the party in power at Westminster.

As has already been discussed in Chapter 5, the Advocate General for Scotland, who is a Law Officer of the UK Parliament, has the power, under section 33(1) of the Act, to refer the question as to whether a Bill or any provision of a Bill is within the legislative competence of the Scottish Parliament to the Judicial Committee of the Privy Council for decision. This approach dictates that the final decision is made by judges.

In some circumstances a political, rather than a judicial, approach is considered appropriate. Secretaries of State of the UK Parliament have the power under section 35 to make an order prohibiting the Presiding Officer from submitting a Bill for Royal Assent under certain circumstances.[4]

Similarly, under section 58, a Secretary of State may prevent a member of the Scottish Executive from taking a proposed action or may require such a member to take action under certain circumstances. The circumstances cover situations where a UK Minister has reasonable grounds for believing that a member of the Scottish Executive is about to act in a way which is incompatible with any international obligation. On the other hand, if he believes that some action is required for giving effect to an international obligation, a Secretary of State can direct by order that the action be taken by a member of the Scottish Executive. Such an action might even include

---

[2] Section 35.

[3] See Chapter 4 of *Scotland's Parliament*, particularly paras 4.4 and 4.15. It should be noted that notwithstanding this optimistic expectation, the changes in Scots law which were brought about by the Asylum and Immigration Act 1999 were strongly criticised by some opposition MSPs as an example of the Westminster Parliament legislating in areas which had otherwise been devolved.

[4] See Chapter 5.

introducing a Bill in the Scottish Parliament although it is difficult to see how MSPs, particularly those from political parties different from that of the UK Government, could be forced to vote for such a Bill. In that case, the UK Government would probably fall back on the power of the UK Parliament, in section 28(7), to make laws for Scotland and pass the Bill themselves. Such a situation would lead to a serious political confrontation between the two governments and, no doubt, strenuous endeavours would be made behind the scenes to avoid such a crisis.

Section 58 also gives Secretaries of State the power to revoke subordinate legislation made by a member of the Scottish Executive which is considered to be incompatible with an international obligation, or the interests of defence or national security, or which makes modifications to the law as it relates to reserved matters that would have an adverse effect on the operation of the law in question. An order made under section 58 must contain reasons.

In addition, there are powers shared between UK Ministers of the Crown and Scottish Ministers[5] which require to be handled by liaison arrangements. Functions in relation to the observation and implementation of European Community rights and rights under the European Convention on Human Rights continue in the main to be dealt with by UK Ministers.[6] As a backstop, the UK Parliament retains the power to make adjustments to the powers of the Scottish Parliament by amending the Scotland Act.

LIAISON ARRANGEMENTS

If the various executive and legislative controls described above were to be used on a frequent basis, that would be an indication that the devolution settlement was under strain. The clear hope of the Government when it launched its proposals for a Scottish Parliament was that a good working relationship between the UK Government and the Scottish Executive would allow areas of difficulty to be dealt with at an early stage, through joint working, consultation, and other more informal mechanisms, and thereby avoid the need for what would almost inevitably be a controversial use by central government of its ultimate executive and legislative supremacy. In order to put such arrangements on a firm footing, the UK Government has entered into a number of agreements with the Scottish Ministers (and the other devolved administrations in the UK) which seek to set out the terms on which the different administrations will work together, at both political and official levels.[7]

---

[5]Conferred by section 56. See Chapter 5.
[6]Section 57.
[7]See *Devolution: memorandum of understanding and supplementary agreements between the United Kingdom Government, Scottish Ministers and the Cabinet of National Assembly of Wales*, Cm 4444 (Stationery Office, 1999). This contains the underlying agreement together with the first 'concordats' (see below, p 86). See http://www.scotland.gov.uk/memorandum.

Although the texts establishing these arrangements described them as "agreements", it should be noted that it is clearly stated that the agreements should not be legally binding. It is also clear that the agreements are not intended to give either the various administrations who are signatories to them, nor indeed any other individual or corporate person, any rights which they can enforce through legal proceedings. They are instead statements of principle, intended to be "binding in honour only". Notwithstanding their non-binding nature, however, the various agreements are likely to be of great practical significance in setting down the basis on which the devolved administrations will work with the UK Government. Moreover, the very terminology of the agreements is clearly designed to give them a special status, marking them out as having a constitutional significance beyond the ordinary government document. Indeed, although the agreements make it clear that they do not create new legal rights and obligations, one might well expect that in due course attempts might well be made in court proceedings to suggest that they can at least be used to provide a background against which a particular action of a Minister can be judged.

The main elements of these arrangements are now described.

The principal agreement is the Memorandum of Understanding which sets out the principles that are to underlie relations between the UK Government, and the devolved administrations, and contains a number of important provisions.

- It commits the various administrations to seek to alert each other to relevant developments within their areas of responsibility; to give appropriate consideration to the views of each other's administration; and, where appropriate, to establish arrangements that allow for policies where there is shared responsibility to be drawn up jointly between the administrations.
- It makes provisions for the exchange of information, statistics and research.
- It places on each of the administrations a responsibility to respect any confidentiality restrictions imposed by the provider of any information.
- It affirms as a convention that the UK Parliament would not normally legislate on devolved matters without the agreement of the devolved legislature. However, the UK Parliament retains the right to discuss any devolved matter, and similarly the Scottish Parliament, and the other devolved assemblies, will be entitled to debate non-devolved matters.
- It affirms that the legal controls over the Scottish Parliament and the other devolved assemblies are only to be used by the UK Government as a last resort.

The Memorandum also established a Joint Ministerial Committee. This comprises the UK Prime Minister, the Scottish and Northern Ireland First Ministers, the Welsh First Secretary (together in all cases with a deputy or other colleague) and the Secretaries of State for

Northern Ireland, Scotland, and Wales, together with other members of the various administrations as appropriate. It is to meet in this structure on a plenary basis at least once a year. In addition, the Joint Ministerial Committee may meet in other "functional" formats: for example, if dealing with environment issues, it will be comprised of the relevant Environment Ministers, and if agriculture, the relevant Agriculture Ministers.

The Joint Ministerial Committee is to meet for two purposes: first, to take stock of the way that devolution is working, either generally or in a particular area, and, second, to deal with particular problems between two or more administrations (if other attempts to resolve them have been unsuccessful). The committee is staffed by a Joint Secretariat, and is shadowed by a committee of officials from the various administrations. The Secretariat and Committee will prepare matters for meetings, and also allow for contact and discussion at official level on the way that the devolution arrangements are working, again both in general terms and in the context of any particular difficulty that might arise. It will no doubt be the case that an effort will be made to resolve potential differences between the various administrations at official level in the Secretariat, or the committee of officials, rather than require them to be discussed by the Joint Ministerial Committee itself.

Accompanying the Memorandum and the Joint Ministerial Committee are the Concordats, which seek to set out detailed working arrangements between the different administrations. Four Concordats were drawn up shortly after the elections to the Scottish Parliament and the National Assembly for Wales, to deal with matters affecting all the devolved administrations, with the aim of providing a broadly similar framework applicable for them all. These cover the following areas of government activity:

- Co-ordination of European Union Policy Issues
- Financial Assistance to Industry
- International Relations
- Statistics.

In addition to these broad-ranging concordats, it was also agreed that bilateral concordats be set up between individual UK Government departments and their Scottish and Welsh counterparts to deal with working relationships on a more detailed basis, and a large number of such agreements have been drawn up. Such agreements can be entered into by two or more administrations as and when they are required, and no doubt as time goes by new issues will arise which will result in new concordats being put in place.

These various arrangements are backed up by a Guidance Note on Common Working Arrangements, dealing with matters such as the way in which bilateral relations between different administrations should be conducted, correspondence, dealing with parliamentary business when they concern the responsibility of a different Parliament or Assembly, and the notification of legislative proposals. The Note also points out that although concordats are to regulate many working relationships between different administrations, other, less formal, arrangements (or just *ad hoc* arrangements) will be appropriate in many cases.

In addition to these arrangements, it should also be noted that the Secretary of State for Scotland (as with the other territorial Secretaries of State) provides a channel of communication between the UK Government and the Scottish Executive at the highest level. Indeed, the Memorandum of Understanding gives these Secretaries of State a specific role in trying to resolve differences between the UK Government and a devolved administration before it requires to be considered by the Joint Ministerial Committee. Furthermore, there are many reserved matters of major importance to Scotland, and it will be for the Secretary of State to represent Scotland's interests in such areas.

FINANCIAL CONTROLS

The financing of the Scottish Parliament is dealt with in detail in Chapter 8. Suffice it to say at this point that the UK Government and Parliament retain tight financial controls over the Scottish Parliament. Most of the Scottish Parliament's expenditure is financed by a block grant determined annually by the Treasury. The Treasury also has the power to require the Scottish Ministers to provide any information it may reasonably ask for.

The Scottish Parliament has only very limited tax-raising powers, powers which are as strictly, if not more, constrained than the tax-raising powers of local government. The Scotland Act describes these as "tax–varying" powers. The Parliament has the power, under section 73, to vary the rate of income tax paid by Scottish taxpayers upwards or downwards by three pence in the £. At current rates this means an increase or decrease in the monies available of only about £700 million. The Scotland Act requires the Scottish Parliament to make provision by legislation for financial control, accounts and audit[8] and one of the first measures introduced into the Parliament was a Bill to deal with such matters.[9]

THE OFFICE OF THE SECRETARY OF STATE FOR SCOTLAND

The office of the Secretary of State for Scotland has a long history, dating back to the days before the union of the Scottish and English Parliaments in 1707. After the Jacobite rebellion of 1745, the office lapsed in the following year and the Lord Advocate became the chief Scottish Minister. This arrangement lasted until 1885 when the office of Secretary for Scotland and a Scottish Office were re-established. In 1892 the Secretary for Scotland was given a seat in the Cabinet and

---

[8] Section 70.

[9] *Public Finance and Accountability (Scotland) Act 2000*, introduced in the Parliament on 7th September 1999, and enacted 17th January 2000.

has retained that seat ever since except in time of war. In 1926, the title was changed to that of Secretary of State for Scotland. In 1939, St Andrew's House in Edinburgh was opened as the headquarters of the Scottish Office and the powers of the Scottish Office were directly vested in the Secretary of State.

There are many references to the Secretary of State in the Scotland Act. As has been explained above,[10] the offices of Secretary of State are interchangeable and in some cases the powers conferred by the Scotland Act will be exercisable by other Ministers of the Crown. However, the Secretary of State for Scotland was given many important powers to be exercised in the seven months between the passing of the Scotland Act and the formal opening of the Scottish Parliament by the Queen on 1st July 1999, for example, the date of the first election and the day, time and place for the first meeting of the Parliament after the poll.[11] A large number of orders were made by the Secretary of State for Scotland during that interim period.[12] On 1st July 1999, the Parliament received its full legislative powers and most of the powers of the Secretary of State were transferred to the Scottish Executive. From that date, the role of the Secretary of State was undoubtedly diminished, although the first holder of that office thereafter, John Reid, has vigorously emphasised the continuing importance of the Secretary of the State in Scotland's public life. The Scottish Office was "re-branded" as the Scotland Office, and the Secretary of State has continued to be a figure of major political influence in Scotland. Nevertheless, the size of the ministerial team was cut to reflect the reduced legislative and executive powers over Scottish matters remaining with the UK Government and Parliament. Although the Secretary of State continues to have important responsibilities to act as a channel of communication between the Scottish Parliament and its Executive, and the UK Parliament and Government, and to look after Scottish interests in reserved matters, it is hard to believe that the relative importance of the Secretary of State *vis-à-vis* both the Scottish Executive and other UK Cabinet Ministers will not decline as devolution becomes established. There was speculation before the elections to the Scottish Parliament that given the constitutional changes taking place in Wales, Northern Ireland, and London (and indeed also in the UK Parliament itself), as well as Scotland, the respective Secretaries of State might be replaced by one new Cabinet post — perhaps a Secretary of State for Constitutional Affairs — with liaison arrangements with the devolved institutions being handled by Ministers below Cabinet rank. However, no doubt for reasons of practical politics, and also the continued uncertainties of the Northern Ireland peace process, all three Secretaries of State have retained their places in the Cabinet so far, and there is no indication that the UK

---

[10]See Chapter 6 above.

[11]Section 2.

[12]Indeed, the Secretary of State continued to make orders under the transitional provisions of the Scotland Act even *after* the first elections to the Parliament on a number of matters prior to the Parliament making its own legislation in the area concerned.

Government intends to change that position, at least in the short term.

CHALLENGING AN ACT OF THE SCOTTISH PARLIAMENT AND SCOTTISH EXECUTIVE ACTIONS

As has been explained in Chapter 2, one of the aspects of the doctrine of the sovereignty of the UK Parliament is that no court of law can find an Act of Parliament to be invalid. The doctrine of Parliamentary sovereignty does not apply to the Scottish Parliament as it is a subordinate body created by statute. It must ensure therefore, that it does not stray beyond the boundaries of the powers conferred on it by statute. In other words, it must act *intra vires*. Any provision in an Act of the Scottish Parliament which is outwith its legislative competence is *ultra vires* and invalid. Quite detailed provisions are made in the Scotland Act to ensure that no Bill introduced into the Scottish Parliament contains any provision which is outwith its legislative competence. These have been discussed in Chapter 5 above. There is always the possibility, however, that such a provision may slip through the net. Legal challenges to the validity of provisions could arise in a wide range of circumstances and might involve disputes between the Scottish Executive and the UK Government, between an individual and the Scottish Executive or between two individuals.

Schedule 6 to the Scotland Act sets out in considerable detail how "devolution issues" are to be handled. A "devolution issue" could arise before virtually any court or tribunal, in civil or in criminal cases. Part 1 of Schedule 6 first defines a devolution issue as "a question whether an Act of the Scottish Parliament or any provision of an Act of the Scottish Parliament is within the legislative competence of the Parliament."

A devolution issue may arise in areas other than Acts of the Scottish Parliament. Questions of legislative competence may arise over the executive actions of Scottish Ministers. Schedule 6 further defines devolution issues as follows:

- a question whether any function is a function of the Scottish Ministers, the First Minister or the Lord Advocate;
- a question whether the purported or proposed exercise of a function by a member of the Scottish Executive is, or would be, within devolved competence;
- a question whether a purported or proposed exercise of a function by a member of the Scottish Executive is, or would be, incompatible with any rights under the European Convention on Human Rights or with European Community law;
- a question whether a failure to act by a member of the Scottish Executive is incompatible with any of the rights under the European Convention of Human Rights or with European Community law;
- any other question about whether a function is exercisable

within devolved competence in or as regards Scotland and any other question arising by virtue of the Scotland Act about reserved matters.

However, a devolution issue is not to be taken to arise in any legal proceedings just because one of the parties argues that it does if the court considers that contention to be "frivolous or vexatious".[13]

HUMAN RIGHTS LEGISLATION AND THE SCOTLAND ACT

An interesting feature of the Scotland Act was that its provisions requiring legislation, and actions of the Scottish Executive (including, of course, actions of those acting on behalf of its members) to be compatible with the European Convention on Human Rights came into effect when the Scottish Parliament and the members of the Scottish Executive acquired their respective powers in stages in mid-1999. By contrast, the date when the Human Rights Act 1998, which incorporated "Convention rights" into UK law, was to come into force was delayed until almost a year and half later. To allow for the fact that the Human Rights Act was expected to come into force after the provisions of the Scotland Act did so, the latter laid down that the Convention rights as provided for in the Human Rights Act would apply to the relevant sections of the Scotland Act *as if* the Human Rights Act were in force.[14] The practical effect of these provisions is that the Convention rights became incorporated into Scots law as far as devolved matters were concerned as soon as executive and legislative powers were transferred to the Scottish Parliament and Executive in the summer of 1999. The significant consequence of the partial incorporation of Convention rights in this way has been that, although a large number of devolution issues have arisen in Scottish courts since the relevant provisions of the Scotland Act came into force, with very few exceptions such questions have related to human rights issues (the vast majority relating to the criminal law).

It may be that when the Human Rights Act comes fully into force such issues will no longer be raised as devolution issues, but as questions arising directly from the provisions of the Human Rights Act. There is some uncertainty as to whether the coming into force of the Human Rights Act will mean that any challenges to Scottish legislation, or the actions of members of the Scottish Executive, can be based *only* on the provisions of that Act, or whether it will be possible to raise "human rights issues" where they concern devolved matters *both* under that Act *and* the Scotland Act (with important implications both for procedure and the remedies which the courts can grant in the event of a breach of a "Convention right").

---

[13]Schedule 6, para 2.
[14]Section 129(2)

LEGAL PROCEEDINGS IN SCOTLAND

Part 2 of Schedule 6 deals with legal proceedings in Scotland. (Legal proceedings in England and Wales are dealt with in Part 3, and in Northern Ireland in Part 4.) Proceedings may be instituted by the Advocate General, *i.e.* the UK Government's Law Officer for Scotland, or the Lord Advocate. The Lord Advocate may defend proceedings instituted by the Advocate General. A court or tribunal must order intimation of any devolution issue arising before it to the Lord Advocate and the Advocate General and they may take part as a party in the proceedings so far as they relate to a devolution issue.

In civil proceedings before a lower court (*i.e.* the Sheriff Court or the Outer House of the Court of Session) or a tribunal, a devolution issue which arises may be referred to the Inner House of the Court of Session. A tribunal from which there is no right of appeal *must* make such a reference. In criminal proceedings before the District Courts, the Sheriff Court or before a single judge in the High Court a devolution issue, if it arises, may be referred to a larger bench of judges in the High Court of Justiciary. A comprehensive set of rules has been brought into effect specifying how devolution issues are to be raised in both the lower courts and the Scottish appeal courts, and how appeals from the lower courts should be dealt with.[15]

Any court consisting of three or more judges of the Court of Session (normally a civil appeal court) or two or more judges of the High Court of Justiciary (a court of criminal appeal) may refer a devolution issue to the Judicial Committee of the Privy Council, unless the issue has been referred to either of them by a lower court in which case the issue must be decided by the superior court. Where the Court of Session has decided a devolution issue referred to it by a lower court, an *appeal* lies to the Judicial Committee.

There are two courts in Scotland from which there is normally no further appeal to the House of Lords. These are the High Court of Justiciary, sitting as a court of criminal appeal, and the Lands Valuation Appeal Court. If a decision on a devolution issue has been made by one of these courts, an appeal may be made to the Judicial Committee with the leave of the court concerned or with special leave of the Judicial Committee. Not surprisingly, given that the Judicial Committee can only decide on a devolution issue on appeal or reference from another court, no such issues had reached it before the end of 1999. However, the indications are that cases will be likely to start coming before it from early 2000.[16]

It is perhaps appropriate to mention here the composition of the Judicial Committee for the purposes of legal proceedings under

---

[15] Act of Adjournal (Devolution Issues Rules) 1999 (SI 1999/1346 (S. 101) (for criminal matters); Act of Sederunt (Devolution Issues Rules) 1999 (SI 1999/1345 (S. 100) (for civil matters, Court of Session); Act of Sederunt (Proceedings for Determination of Devolution Issues Rules) 1999 (SI 1999/1347 (S. 102)) (for civil matters, Sheriff Court).

[16] Rules of procedure have been already made by order for such appeals and references: the Judicial Committee (Devolution Issues) Rules Order 1999 (SI 1999/665).

the Scotland Act. The Committee currently consists of 109 members, of whom 52 come from Commonwealth countries. There are only two women. The average age is 67. Section 103 of the Scotland Act states that no member of the Judicial Committee shall sit and act in legal proceedings involving devolution issues unless he is a Law Lord or has held what is described as "high judicial office" defined in the Appellate Jurisdiction Act of 1876. This has the effect of excluding the Commonwealth members.

If a devolution issue arises in judicial proceedings in the House of Lords, it is to be referred to the Judicial Committee unless the House of Lords considers it more appropriate to determine the issue themselves.

The Law Officers of Scotland, England and Northern Ireland may require a court or tribunal before which a devolution issue has arisen to refer it to the Judicial Committee. A direct reference to the Judicial Committee may also be made by the Law Officers of Scotland, England and Northern Ireland of a devolution issue which is *not* the subject of legal proceedings. This will involve the judges in ruling on hypothetical issues, rather than on concrete facts, an extremely unusual procedure for British judges.

Any decision of the Judicial Committee in proceedings under the Scotland Act is to be stated in open court and is to be binding in all legal proceedings except those before the Judicial Committee itself.[17] This would appear to be a fairly unusual example of statute laying down rules of judicial precedent which must be followed by judges sitting in courts below the Judicial Committee.

The Act also includes a provision for subordinate legislation to be made by a UK Minister to remedy *ultra vires* provisions in Acts of the Scottish Parliament.[18] Such subordinate legislation may also be made to remedy any improper exercise of functions by Scottish Ministers. Such subordinate legislation may be retrospective in effect.[19] This can remedy any problems which have arisen and put third parties into the position they thought they were in before the flaw in the Act or subordinate legislation was discovered. There is a further provision in section 102 which allows any court or tribunal to remove, limit or suspend any retrospective effect of their decision that a provision of an Act of the Scottish Parliament or subordinate legislation is *ultra vires*. One of the criteria the court or tribunal must take into account in making an order under this section is the extent to which persons not party to the proceedings would otherwise be adversely affected. The Lord Advocate and any other appropriate Law Officer must be given notice of an intention to make such an order and the opportunity to be party to the proceedings as they relate to the order.

The Scottish Parliament is not the first experiment in devolution in the UK. After the partition of Ireland, a Northern Ireland Parliament was established in 1921 and continued in existence until 1972. By and

---

[17]Section 103.
[18]Section 107.
[19]Section 114(3).

large the Members of that Parliament were content with the powers which had been conferred. They tried to avoid constitutional tension by seeking the co-operation of the UK Parliament and generally found co-operation there. The courts were rarely called upon to resolve disputes. Although a number of challenges were made only one had much success.[20] However, the political and religious circumstances in Northern Ireland were, and still are, very different from those in Scotland. Only time will tell whether Scottish devolution will keep the courts busier than they were in Northern Ireland.

---

[20]*Ulster Transport Authority* v. *James Brown & Son Ltd* [1953] NI 79.

8. FINANCING THE SCOTTISH PARLIAMENT

INTRODUCTION

The two principal sources of finance for the Scottish Parliament and the Scottish Administration are the "block grant" allocated to it by the UK Government and Parliament, and a supplement to UK income tax to be paid by Scottish taxpayers. If it so wishes, the Parliament will also be able to reduce the level of income tax to be paid by such taxpayers, with a corresponding reduction in the level of finance available to it.

THE BLOCK GRANT

In *Scotland's Parliament*, the Government made it clear that it envisaged that the main source of finance for the Parliament would be the block grant. The block grant is a grant paid by the UK Treasury to the Scottish Office. The level of the block grant is decided from year to year in accordance with a formula which decides the balance of government spending between Scotland, England and Wales. This is known as the "Barnett formula", named after Chief Secretary to the Treasury in 1978 when the formula was devised to take account of the plans for devolution at that time. The Barnett formula took account of the fact that at the time it was devised, government spending was relatively higher in Scotland (and Wales) than in England. The formula aimed, at least in theory, to bring about a gradual convergence between the relative levels of government spending in Scotland, Wales, and England. In fact, primarily due to the fact that Scotland's share of the total Great Britain population is declining, that convergence has not taken place.[1]

Although there have been suggestions from time to time that there should be some independent method of deciding the appropriate level of government grant to Scotland in relation to that of other parts of the UK,[2] no such provision has yet been adopted. The Scotland Act has nothing to say about the level of the block grant, or how the level of government expenditure in Scotland should relate to that of the rest of the UK. The current block grant, decided in the light of the Barnett formula, will therefore continue to be the main constituent of

---

[1]After the 1992 General Election, the formula was revised to a limited extent by Michael Portillo (then Chief Secretary to the Treasury). Also see *Scotland's Parliament: Fundamentals for a New Scotland Act* (Constitution Unit, 1996) for a useful discussion of the financial arrangements for devolution.

[2]Ibid Chapter 5.

the finance available to the new Parliament and the Scottish Government.

As the level of grant and the formula are left to the UK Government and Parliament, the Scotland Act requires to make only limited provision to allow the current system to be applied to the new Parliament. It simply establishes a Scottish Consolidated Fund, and gives to the Secretary of State the powers to make payments into that Fund "out of money provided by [the UK] Parliament of such amounts as he may determine."[3] The Secretary of State will presumably make such payments in line with the Barnett formula until and unless the UK Government decides on a different basis for the allocation of funds to Scotland.

The Act specifically restricts the powers of the Scottish Executive to borrow money, which means that neither it nor the Parliament can circumvent the limited powers to vary taxes by attempting to borrow money for its programmes. The Scottish Ministers have a limited power to borrow money from the Secretary of State to cover a *temporary* shortfall in the Scottish Consolidated Fund, or to provide a working balance in that fund. Otherwise, they can only borrow money under the authority of an Act of the UK Parliament.[4]

As one would expect, the Act also contains a number of arrangements primarily of a technical nature to ensure that the Scottish Parliament and Executive use the finances available to them in a proper manner. Money may only be paid out of the Scottish Consolidated Fund for expenditure for which the Act or other legislation gives authority.[5] The Act obliged the Scottish Parliament to introduce legislation requiring the Scottish Ministers to prepare accounts of their income and expenditure, and to lay accounts and report on them before the Parliament. Legislation to that effect, the Public Finance and Accountability (Scotland) Act 2000, which received the Royal Assent on 17th January 2000, was passed early in the life of the Parliament. Its provisions include the establishment of Audit Scotland, which provides a single public sector audit service, comprising existing staff of the Accounts Commission for Scotland and the Scottish staff of the National Audit Office. The Scotland Act also provided for the appointment by the Crown, on the nomination of the Scottish Parliament, of an Auditor-General for Scotland, with duties which include the responsibility to examine and report on the accounts of income and expenditure of the Scottish Executive. The first Auditor-General for Scotland was nominated in September 1999.[6] The Auditor General for Scotland also has a duty to examine the "economy, efficiency, and effectiveness" with which the Scottish Ministers, the Lord Advocate, or any other person or organisation who has received money from the Scottish Consolidated Fund, have

---

[3]Section 64.
[4]Section 66.
[5]Section 65.
[6]The person appointed, Robert Black, was at the time the current Controller of Audit.

used the funds available to them.[7] Accordingly, the Public Finance and Accountability (Scotland) Act gives the Auditor-General for Scotland the power to commission financial audit and value for money studies across much of the public sector in Scotland. The audit of local authorities, however, will continue to be supervised by the Accounts Commission for Scotland, and their audit reports will not be submitted to the Parliament. (As the Accounts Commission's staff are transferred by the Scottish legislation to Audit Scotland, it will require to use that body's services to carry out this supervisory function.)

The Act also contains a transitional provision which applies in cases where the Secretary of State has lent funds from the UK National Loans Fund prior to the establishment of the Parliament. If the power under which the Secretary of State had made such loans has been transferred to the Scottish Ministers, any repayment of capital or interest on the loan will now be paid to the Scottish Ministers and the Scottish Consolidated Fund, and a matching adjustment to be made in the sums payable by the Secretary of State to the Scottish Ministers.[8]

THE POWER TO VARY INCOME TAX

By contrast with the limited number of provisions allowing a block grant to be paid to the new Scottish Government, the arrangements set out in the Act to allow the Parliament to raise its own taxes are comprehensive. That had to be so, as the power to levy taxes is one of the powers which are otherwise reserved to the UK Parliament.[9]

The power to raise taxes is contained in Part IV of the Act. The power allows the Parliament to increase or decrease the basic rate of UK tax for "Scottish taxpayers". The maximum that the Parliament can so vary the basic tax rate is three pence in the pound, but the Parliament can vary the tax rate by a lesser amount if it wishes. The variation can only be for whole or half pennies. If the Parliament wishes to use the power, it has to pass a resolution to that effect for each year it wishes to do so. It should be noted that the maximum variation is not linked to the actual level at which the basic tax rate is set for the UK in any one year. That means that the proportionate effect of a Scottish variation on the total basic tax rate may vary significantly from year to year. For example, if the basic tax rate is 20 pence in the pound, a three pence variation would mean a variation in the tax rate of 15 per cent. If the basic rate were 30 pence in the pound, the variation in the tax rate would be only 10 per cent.

It will be seen that the tax varying power only applies to "Scottish taxpayers". Accordingly, the Act requires to define such a person, and does so in a complex set of provisions set out in section 75. The Act should be referred to it for its precise provisions, but the basic

---

[7] Section 70.
[8] Section 71.
[9] Schedule 5, Part II, s. A1.

definition is as follows[10]: a Scottish taxpayer is an individual who in the relevant year is resident for income tax purposes in the UK *and* Scotland is the part of the UK with which he has the "closest connection" in that year.

Such an individual has such a "closest connection" if:

(i) the number of days which he or she spends in Scotland in that year is equal to or exceeds the number of days spent elsewhere in the United Kingdom *and/or*

(ii) he or she (a) spends at least part of the relevant year in Scotland; *and* (b) for at least part of the time spent in Scotland, his or her principal UK home is in Scotland and he or she makes use of it as a place of residence; *and* (c) the total time in that year that such a person's principal UK home is in Scotland is as least as much as the times when his or her principal UK home is not in Scotland.

The Act seeks to give definitions of what is meant by "spending a day" and "principal UK home".

The purpose of the definition is to ensure that all those who might reasonably be regarded as Scottish taxpayers are liable to the tax, without catching also more transient persons such as the occasional holiday visitor. It seeks to deal with some of the possible anomalies which might arise if the Scottish Parliament does indeed exercise its powers to vary the basic tax rate from that levied in England. So, for example, a person who lives in Dumfries, but travels every day to work in Carlisle, will normally be a Scottish taxpayer (although that person's colleagues may well be paying a different tax rate if they live in Carlisle); and a person who lives in Edinburgh, but commutes each week to work (and stays overnight) in London from Monday to Friday, will usually still be regarded as a Scottish taxpayer. However, a person who normally resides outside Scotland, but who has a holiday home in Scotland, will in most situations not qualify as a Scottish taxpayer. (In addition, a member of the Scottish Parliament, or a UK or European MP representing a Scottish constituency will automatically be regarded as having his or her "closest connection" with Scotland).

There are a number of other important features about the arrangements made in the Act for the use of the power to vary income tax.

- a "Scottish taxpayer" is defined as being an *individual*[11];
- income from savings and distributions, as defined in section 73 of the Act, is excluded from income to which the tax-varying power applies (so that any such income will not be liable to any increase in tax if a Scottish Parliament uses its power to raise taxes[12];

---

[10]For some comments on the operation of the tax varying power, see Sandra Eden, "Taxing Times Ahead for the Scots" (1998) Scots Law Times (News) 57.

[11]So sole traders and partners in firms will be liable to pay the varied rate of tax, but "non-natural persons" will not.

[12]Amongst the types of income that *will* normally be covered are wages and salaries from employment, most pensions, and the profits of a trade or profession, and the profits from land.

- a proposal that the tax-varying power should be used can only be put to the Parliament by a member of the Scottish Executive (and so the power could not be used at the instigation of an opposition party, or an individual back-bench MP).

One problem with the tax-varying power which was identified in the debate prior to introduction of the Scotland Bill was that as it was linked to the basic rate of tax, the extent of the tax-varying flexibility open to the Scottish Parliament would be dependent on the UK tax structure. If, for example, the tax banding system used for income tax were to change, the potential of the tax-varying power would also change as a result, as can be seen from the change to the tax bands proposed in the 1999 Budget. Given that there has been a move in recent years to extend the impact of the lower rate taxation band, together with debate about more substantial tax reforms, it was felt by many commentators that the tax-varying powers of the Scottish Parliament should be flexible enough to cope with that eventuality. Section 76 of the Act attempts to deal with these concerns. It provides that if a proposed change to the income tax structure is such as to "have a significant effect on the practical extent ... of the Parliament's tax-varying powers", the UK Treasury is required to put a statement before the House of Commons as to whether in its opinion a consequential variation of those tax-varying powers is required, and if so to make proposals for amending those powers accordingly. Any such proposal must be restricted to income tax (maintaining the exemption for income from savings and distributions), and any such amendment must be to the general effect that the tax-varying powers should remain "broadly the same" as if it had been in force in 1997/8. In addition, any such amendment must not result in a "significant difference" to the after-tax income of Scottish taxpayers.

Although the provisions for the use of the tax-varying power are comprehensively set out in the Act, it remains to be seen what practical use will be made of those powers. If the block grant remains at current levels, the impact of the tax varying power even if fully utilised will be minimal by comparison. In the White Paper, *Scotland's Parliament*, the Government considered[13] that the sum which would be raised in Scotland by increasing the basic rate of tax by three pence would be £450 million. (This figure increased to £690 million as a result of the 1999 Budget.) These figures represent 3–5 per cent of the total funding provided by the block grant, which puts its significance into proportion.

Moreover, there would be costs incurred in setting up the system to vary income tax. In the White Paper, *Scotland's Parliament*, the Government estimated that the cost to government and employers combined in setting up the necessary system to vary the basic rate tax would initially be in the region of £60 million, and that the running costs thereafter would be between £14 and £23 million per year (others have suggested that the costs might be higher). Given the

---

[13]Para 7.13.

relatively high cost of collection of the extra tax set against its potential yield (particularly if the power to vary taxes was not to be utilised to its full extent), it may be that there will be some reluctance amongst the Scottish political parties to use these powers. The Scottish Labour Party has stated that it will not use the tax-varying powers, at least in the initial years of the Parliament and that commitment was incorporated into the agreement between the Scottish Labour and Liberal Democrat parties establishing the coalition government after the first elections to the Parliament. In its election manifesto for those elections, the SNP restricted itself to a proposed use of the tax-raising power to the extent of a one penny increase only, and given the outcome of those elections, there is uncertainty as to whether the SNP would enter a future election with a commitment to raise income tax at all. There certainly seems to be little prospect of the tax–varying power being used in the early years of the Parliament.

LOCAL TAXATION AND THE PARLIAMENT

It was mentioned above that the taxes and excise duties were matters which were generally reserved to the UK Parliament. That is why the Act has to give specific powers to the Scottish Parliament to have the tax-varying power described above. However, the Act does make clear that notwithstanding this general reservation of taxation, the Scottish Parliament *will* be able to legislate to make changes, if it so wishes, to the system of local taxation to fund local authority expenditure.[14] Council tax and non-domestic rates are given as specific examples of such local taxation on which the Parliament will be able to legislate.

The Parliament has therefore been given broad powers to reform local taxation if it so wishes. It can make changes to the way that the present system is administered, for example, by changing the banding system for council tax. It could decide whether to retain the ability to set a level for the non-domestic rate (the "business rate") on a Scotland-wide basis, or to leave local councils to determine its level. If it retains the ability to fix the business rate, it could decide the level at which it should be fixed. The Parliament can also decide whether to impose any "cap" on the spending of local councils. The Parliament can also introduce fundamental reforms to the system of local government finance (*e.g.* funding local government by a land tax, or the introduction of a tourist tax.) It is suggested that the new forms of local taxation which could be introduced by the Parliament could even include a local sales tax, or indeed local income tax, although in practice such changes could probably only be brought about with the consent of the UK Parliament, as they would probably only be practicable if the UK sales and income taxes systems were modified to make the collection of such a tax possible. (It can be expected that any attempt to set up

---

[14]Schedule 5, s. A1.

systems for collection of local sales taxes or income taxes which were separate from the UK VAT and income tax systems would be inordinately expensive and constitute an unwanted administrative burden for Scottish business. A local sales tax might conflict with EC rules.) Notwithstanding the powers available to it, however, the first government formed in May 1999 has made it clear that it does not intend to carry out any changes to the system of local taxation, and will retain the power to set a Scotland-wide uniform business rate.

As a substantial proportion of the finance provided by the block grant is then passed on to local government to support the services that it provides, the theoretical possibility exists that even with the restricted tax-varying powers available to it, the Scottish Parliament could increase the real resources available to it by the device of reducing the sums it pays to local government. As a result, it would be able to retain a bigger share of the block grant, and local councils would have to meet the shortfall in resources either by cutting services or increasing local taxation. By such means, the Scottish Parliament could in effect increase its tax raising powers by making use in an indirect manner of the taxation powers available to local government. However, although there are no specific provisions in the Act to meet such an eventuality, the government clearly had in mind when it launched its proposals for Scottish devolution that some controls over local government expenditure might be required. Consequently, it is stated in *Scotland's Parliament*[15] that if there were to be growth in the "self-financed" expenditure of local councils which could be considered "excessive and were such as to threaten targets set for public expenditure as management of the UK economy ... it would be open to the UK Government to take the excess into account in considering the level of their support for expenditure in Scotland" if the Scottish Parliament chose not to take steps to reduce that growth in expenditure. In blunt terms, that would mean that if local councils increased local taxes, either because of their own decisions or as a result of reduction in grant support from the Scottish Parliament, the UK Government might well reduce the block grant payable to the Parliament. Such a threat would presumably serve as a powerful incentive (as was no doubt intended) to encourage the Scottish Parliament to restrain local government expenditure.

The activities of local government could have an indirect effect on the financial arrangements for a devolved Scotland in another way. At present, central government provides the bulk of the funding for the payments made by local councils as council tax and housing benefit. Under present arrangements, if local councils in Scotland were substantially to increase their levels of council tax and/or housing rent, the effect would be to increase the level of funding from central government. *Scotland's Parliament* makes it clear the resources for these benefits will be included, after devolution, within the block grant, so that if expenditure on these benefits increases as a result of

---

[15]Para 7.24.

decisions taken by Scottish local councils, it will be the Scottish Parliament that will have to find the extra money.[16]

OTHER SOURCES OF FINANCE

The Act places no general restrictions on the Scottish Parliament from introducing charges for services provided by the Scottish Administration, or which other bodies provide on its behalf. Accordingly, it has the power to raise finance in such a way as long as the activity to be supported was one which fell within its general remit. If the level of charge made, however, was such as to raise income in excess of the cost of the provision of the service, it is suggested that the excess amount of the charge might well be regarded as in reality a tax, which would therefore be beyond the powers of the Scottish Parliament to impose (unless it were to fall within the definition of local taxation).

One source of funding which is becoming of increasing importance in a number of areas of government activity which in general fall within the remit of the Scottish Parliament is the National Lottery. "Betting, gaming and lotteries" is a matter reserved to the UK Parliament,[17] so the Scottish Parliament and Executive cannot legislate to establish a Scottish lottery, or have any right to be involved in the management or the disbursement of funds raised by the National Lottery (although some of the bodies which currently have a responsibility for disbursement of lottery funds in Scotland, e.g. the Scottish Arts and Sports Council will come under the authority of the Scottish Parliament and Executive). In addition, one of the Concordats between the Scottish Executive and the UK Government[18] provides for the Scottish Ministers to be given certain powers to make directions and be consulted on appointments to other Lottery distribution bodies. Furthermore, the Annual Reports and Accounts of all the Scottish and UK Lottery distributors except the Millennium Commission, and the Annual Report of the National Lottery Commission, are to be laid before the Scottish Parliament as well as the UK Parliament.

As there are no specific reservations in the Scotland Act preventing the Scottish Executive from obtaining grant aid for its activities, there is presumably no reason why it should not also seek grants from any source that might be prepared to finance its activities.

---

[16]Para 7.25.

[17]Schedule 5, Part II, s. B9.

[18]Concordat between Department for Culture, Media and Sport and the Scottish Executive http://www.scotland.gov.uk/concordats/dcms. See Chapter 7 for discussion on Concordats generally.

9. THE PARLIAMENT, LOCAL GOVERNMENT, AND OTHER PUBLIC BODIES

INTRODUCTION

The relationship between the Parliament and local government deserves special attention as both are tiers of government, elected by a wide popular franchise, accountable through the ballot box and with tax-raising powers. While doing its preparatory work for a Scottish Parliament, the Scottish Constitutional Convention always envisaged that local government would be one of the matters devolved to the Parliament. In its final report, *Scotland's Parliament: Scotland's Right,*[1] the SCC recommended that:

- the relationship between the Parliament and local government should be positive, co-operative and stable;
- the principles of the European Charter of Local Self-Government should be adopted, in particular Article 4 which provides that local authorities should, within the limits of the law, have full discretion to exercise their initiative with regard to any matter which is not excluded from their competence nor assigned to any other authority;
- any future review of Scottish local government should adopt the following aims:
  - (a) to safeguard and where possible increase local authority discretion;
  - (b) to ensure that proposals for reform are widely acceptable in Scotland;
  - (c) to ensure a system of local government finance which sustains local accountability.

Finally it recommended that the Scotland Act should contain a section committing the Parliament to secure and maintain a strong and effective system of local government, embodying the principle of subsidiarity as a guarantee of local government in service delivery.

The White Paper, *Scotland's Parliament*, contained a short chapter on local government and other bodies.[2] It laid out the following general principles:

- the Government does not expect the Scottish Parliament to accumulate a range of new functions at the centre which

---

[1] pp 16–17.
[2] Chapter 6.

would be more appropriately and efficiently delivered by other bodies within Scotland;

- decisions should be made as close as possible to the citizens of Scotland (the principle of subsidiarity);
- the Scottish Parliament should set the national framework within which other Scottish public bodies operate.

On local government in particular, the White Paper made it clear that the Scottish Parliament has general responsibility for legislation and policy relating to local government. It has the power to set the framework within which local government operates and to make changes to its powers, boundaries and functions. The Scottish Executive has responsibility for local government expenditure and for the system of local taxation.

The Scotland Act is virtually silent about the matter of local government but, as has already been discussed, the government opted for the retaining model for the legislation[3] and the only references to local government in Schedule 5[4] which covers reserved matters are to:

- local taxes (which are excepted from reservation); and
- the franchise at local government elections (which is reserved).

It is quite clear, therefore, that all other aspects of local government are devolved to the Scottish Parliament. The Parliament is able to pass legislation on any aspect of local government. It could change the boundaries and the structure completely, although it is unlikely to do so in the near future because of the disruption to the public and to local government employees which a reorganisation entails. It could add functions to, or take functions from, local government and change the way in which services are delivered and how local government is managed. It has responsibility for the financing of local government, both through the system of grants and through determining the form of local taxation.

Scottish Ministers have wide powers to scrutinise the activities of local government either through inspectorates or through bodies such as the Accounts Commission. They have powers to regulate the activities of local government by requiring them to maintain certain standards in, for example, education, social work, law and order. There are also some powers of intervention.

The relationship between the Scottish Parliament and local government is, however, not statutorily defined, despite the recommendation of the Scottish Constitutional Convention, and fears have been expressed by many people working in local government as officers and members that the Scottish Parliament will suck up the powers of local government to itself.

---

[3]See Chapter 3 above.
[4]Schedule 5 covers the matters reserved to the UK Parliament.

THE STRUCTURE AND FUNCTIONS OF LOCAL GOVERNMENT

Before examining the relationship between the Scottish Parliament and local government, it is necessary to give a brief description of the current structure and functions of local government in Scotland. This will make clear the reasons for the fears mentioned above.

Between 1975 and 1996, local government on mainland Scotland was organised on a two-tier basis with nine regional and 53 district councils. There were also three islands councils. The regional councils ranged in population from 2.3 million in Strathclyde Region to 103,000 in the Borders region.[5] The regional councils were responsible for those local government functions which required a relatively large geographical or population base. These included education, police and fire services, social work, roads and transportation, water and sewerage and a number of others including consumer protection.

The district councils ranged in population from 689,000 in Glasgow District to 10,420 in Nairn District. The district councils were responsible for the more local services such as local planning and development control, libraries, museums, parks, refuse collection and disposal, cleansing and environmental health and a wide range of licensing and other regulatory functions. By far the most important and costly function was housing. Because of the sparsity of population in some rural areas, the district councils lying within the Highlands, the Borders and Dumfries and Galloway Regions did not have responsibility for libraries, building control and local planning. Instead these were carried out by the regional councils.

The islands councils for Orkney, Shetland and the Western Isles were treated as special cases and, despite their small populations, were given single-tier most-purpose status. They were responsible for the delivery of virtually all the local government functions with the exception of police and fire which they shared with Highland Regional Council.

The two-tier system of local government was in existence during the discussions on Scottish devolution in the 1970s which culminated in the Scotland Act 1978. That Act was to have established a Scottish Assembly with legislative powers but no powers to raise tax. One of the arguments against devolution at that time was that the establishment of a Scottish Assembly, in addition to the two-tier system of local government, the UK government and the European Parliament (plus community councils in many areas) would lead to Scotland being over-governed. In political terms, it was difficult to envisage how Strathclyde Regional Council, large and powerful, covering more than half the population of Scotland, with an annual budget of around £2.2 billion and local tax-raising powers, could co-exist amicably with a Scottish Assembly which did not have the power to raise even a penny on its own. The Scottish Assembly however, was never established as the threshold in the referendum of March 1979 of

---

[5] 1990 figures.

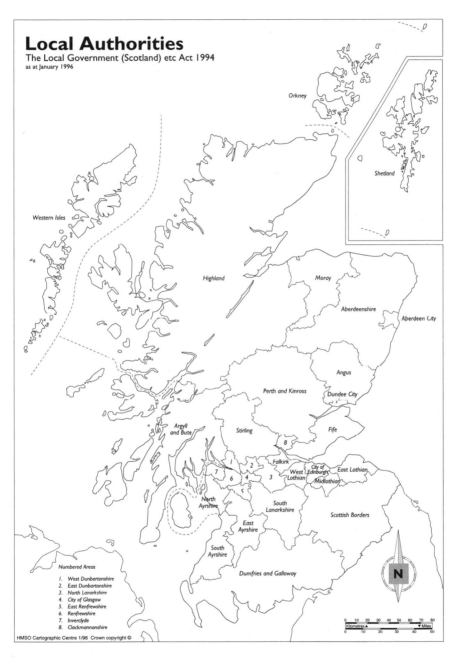

Local Authorities
The Local Government (Scotland) etc Act 1994
as at January 1996

Orkney

Shetland

Western Isles

Highland

Moray

Aberdeenshire

Aberdeen City

Angus

Perth and Kinross

Dundee City

Argyll and Bute

Stirling

Fife

8

Falkirk

West Lothian

City of Edinburgh

East Lothian

Midlothian

North Ayrshire

South Lanarkshire

Scottish Borders

East Ayrshire

South Ayrshire

Dumfries and Galloway

N

Numbered Areas

1. West Dunbartonshire
2. East Dunbartonshire
3. North Lanarkshire
4. City of Glasgow
5. East Renfrewshire
6. Renfrewshire
7. Inverclyde
8. Clackmannanshire

HMSO Cartographic Centre 1/96 Crown copyright ©

Crown copyright is reproduced with the permission of the Controller of Her Majesty's Stationery Office.

40 per cent of the electorate voting "Yes" was not reached.[6] The Conservative Government which was elected in May 1979 repealed the Scotland Act 1978 later that year.

LOCAL GOVERNMENT REORGANISATION

In 1991 the Conservative Government announced, somewhat unexpectedly, that it was their intention to reorganise Scottish local government by abolishing the two-tier system and replacing it with single-tier authorities. In a consultation paper, *The Case for Change*, it was argued that the two-tier system was not readily understood by the public, that it led to a clouding of accountability, and that some of the regions were seen as too large and too remote.[7] It was also argued that the system resulted inevitably in duplication, waste, delays and friction between the two tiers. The case for a single-tier system was basically the mirror image of the criticisms of the two-tier system. It was asserted that it was simple to understand and therefore clarified accountability and that it removed the potential for duplication, waste, delay and friction between the two tiers.[8]

The government's proposals were not welcomed with any enthusiasm in Scotland, least of all by those involved in local government, but the government pressed ahead and passed the Local Government etc. (Scotland) Act 1994. The regional and district councils were abolished on 30th March 1996 and were replaced by 29 single-tier councils on mainland Scotland.[9] The three island councils which had been virtually all-purpose remained unchanged. The 29 new councils came into existence on 1st April 1996 following a "shadow" year during which they co-existed with the regional and district councils. They range in terms of population from Glasgow City Council with 618,430 to Clackmannanshire Council with 48,810. Twelve of the new councils have populations of fewer than 100,000. Because of the small populations of some of the councils, it was not feasible to transfer the entire range of local authority functions to each of the 29 new councils. A council with a population of less than 100,000 is not able to provide, for example, police and fire services on a cost-effective basis. As a result, arrangements were made in the Act for some functions to be removed from local government altogether and for others to be handled on a joint basis by a consortium of councils.

The functions which were removed from local government are:

- water and sewerage — transferred to three Water Authorities whose members are appointed by the Secretary of State for Scotland;
- the children's reporter system — transferred to the Scottish

---

[6] See Chapter 1 above.
[7] *The Structure of Local Government: The Case for Change*, paras 9–10.
[8] Ibid paras 16–17.
[9] See map on p 105.

Children's Reporters Administration whose members are appointed by the Secretary of State for Scotland;
- responsibility for all roads except local roads – transferred to the Scottish Office

The functions handled jointly are:

- police — eight police forces established, six of which are run by joint boards, consisting of representatives of three or more of the new councils. Fife Council has its own police force as does Dumfries and Galloway Council. In the case of Strathclyde Police Force no fewer than 12 councils are involved in the joint board;
- fire services — eight fire brigades established on a basis similar to that for the police forces described above;
- property valuation for council tax and non-domestic rates purposes — run by 10 joint boards. Dumfries and Galloway, Fife, Glasgow, Dundee, and the Scottish Borders Councils are the only councils not involved in joint arrangements;
- structure planning — seventeen structure plan areas established, many of which are run by joint committees;
- public transport — a Strathclyde Passenger Authority established to run public transport in most of the areas of Strathclyde.

Because of the small size of some of the councils, it has been necessary for them to enter into joint arrangements or agency agreements with their neighbours to provide specialist services in, for example, education and social work. A survey carried out by the Convention of Scottish Local Authorities (COSLA) found that between 1996 and 1998 a total of 333 voluntary joint arrangements had been established by Scotland's councils.[10]

Joint committees, boards and other arrangements are not new. There was widespread use of them in Scotland before the introduction of the two-tier system in 1975, when there was a cumbersome structure of over 400 local authorities. Joint arrangements, however, have their drawbacks and have been described as notoriously ineffective. The smaller councils tend to feel dominated by their larger colleagues, they tend to be officer-led rather than member-led and since their members are appointed by the councils and are not directly elected, they lack democratic legitimacy and direct accountability to the electorate.

THE RELATIONSHIP BETWEEN THE SCOTTISH PARLIAMENT AND LOCAL GOVERNMENT

Because of the fragmented nature of local government and the plethora of joint arrangements which now exist, some members and officers see the establishment of the Scottish Parliament as a threat.

---

[10]*COSLA: Voluntary Joint Working Arrangements by Councils 1996/7 and 1997/8.*

They see it as an institution which will further undermine local autonomy. Since certain important services are now carried out under joint boards or committees, the accountability of which is diluted, might the Scottish Parliament, itself directly elected, take control of these services? There has already been discussion of a national police force and a national fire service. Structure planning too might be carried out on a Scottish-wide basis. Although it is unlikely that the Scottish Parliament would want to take control of Scottish schools or social work services, the Parliament certainly has the power to make educational and social work policies. Will these policies be drawn so tightly that local discretion is removed and the local authorities become little more than agents of the Scottish Parliament? There is also the fear that the Parliament, with 129 MSPs, will not provide enough Parliamentary work to keep all its members busy and therefore those without Ministerial office might feel tempted to interfere in the administration of local government functions. This is perhaps most likely to be true of those MSPs who have a background as councillors.

Others take a more optimistic view and see the establishment of the Parliament as an opportunity for a fresh start in which two democratically elected institutions could work in partnership with local government contributing to the development and monitoring of policies.

There has been discussion of the possibility of a concordat, a document which would set out and regulate the relationship between the Parliament and local government. Some see this as a document with the force of law, entrenching the autonomy of local government and preventing the Parliament from encroaching on the traditional powers and functions of councils. Others take the view that the Parliament which has statutory responsibility for all aspects of local government, except the franchise, cannot be prevented from making changes to the framework within which local government operates, as and when circumstances dictate. A concordat could, however, set out a political commitment to the principle of subsidiarity. The UK Government have already given an indication of their commitment to local government by signing and ratifying the European Charter of Local Self-Government shortly after taking office.

THE McINTOSH COMMISSION

Partly in response to the fears expressed above and prior to the passing of the Scotland Act, the Secretary of State for Scotland established a Commission on Local Government and the Scottish Parliament. The Commission was chaired by Neil McIntosh who was the last Chief Executive of Strathclyde Regional Council prior to its abolition in 1996.

Its remit was:

• to consider how to build the most effective relations between local government and the Scottish Parliament and Scottish Executive; and

- to consider how councils can best make themselves responsive and democratically accountable to the communities they serve.

The Commission carried out extensive consultations with interested bodies and presented its final report to the First Minister of the Scottish Executive in June 1999.

Two consultation papers were issued. The first invited comments as to how the relationship between local government (both collectively and at the level of the individual council) and the Scottish Parliament and the Scottish Executive should be established. The second consultation paper commented on responses made to the first paper and posed a series of further questions for consideration. As McIntosh pointed out,[11] it is important to understand the nature of any partnership between central and local government, so that any expectations of that partnership are realistic. Local government is the creature of statute. It is brought into being by an Act of Parliament and can just as easily be abolished by an Act of Parliament. The power to legislate on local government has been devolved to the Scottish Parliament. So the partnership between local government and the Scottish Parliament can never be one of equals since the Parliament ultimately holds power over local government. Nevertheless, it would stand on its head the principle of subsidiarity (that is, that decisions should be taken as closely as possible to those whom they affect) if the Scottish Parliament and Executive were to concentrate the powers traditionally exercised by local government in their own hands. If local government is to be strong and effective as both the Scottish Constitutional Convention and the Government in the White Paper recommended, central government in Edinburgh should not dominate local government.

THE REPORT OF THE McINTOSH COMMISSION

The McIntosh Commission Report on Local Government and the Scottish Parliament was published in June 1999, the month following the first election to the Scottish Parliament.[12] Somewhat surprisingly, the actual relationship between the Scottish Parliament and local government is dealt with in only eight pages. The remainder deal with various other local government issues including the method of election to local councils, the conduct of council business and community councils.

---

[11]Consultation Paper 2, p 8.

[12]*Moving Forward: Local Government and the Scottish Parliament*. The Report of the Commission on Local Government and the Scottish Parliament (The McIntosh Report) June 1999.

The relationship between the Scottish Parliament and local government

The Commission recognises that the establishment of the Parliament represents a fundamental change in the political landscape in which councils operate. Although each has a democratic base, it is the Parliament which has the ultimate power to determine what becomes of local government.

It believes that the principle of subsidiarity should be the key. That principle underlies the Scotland Act which created the Parliament and should be equally applicable to the relationship between the Parliament and local government. If a greater centralisation of power is proposed, the onus of proof should be on those who propose centralisation to demonstrate that it will bring greater benefit to the public at large. Since both have a common democratic basis, relations between local government and the Parliament should be on the basis of mutual respect and parity of esteem.

However, McIntosh asserts that to earn that parity of esteem, the Parliament will have to be convinced that it is dealing with local authorities which are as responsive to and as representative of their electorates as possible and which are ready and willing to embrace renewal in their attitudes and working practices. Certain principles drawn from those laid down for the Parliament are set out:

- accountability;
- accessibility, transparency, responsiveness and a participative approach;
- equal opportunities for all.

These are further developed into:

- participation by the citizen;
- transparency in the conduct of council business;
- focus on the customer;
- delivery of quality and cost-effective services;
- partnership working;
- improvement of the public image;
- promotion of active citizenship and social inclusion;
- good employment practices.

Although many of these are to be found in local government at present, McIntosh warns that if local government does not deliver to the Parliament's satisfaction, the Parliament will look elsewhere — perhaps to quangos, accountable to Ministers, and local government will find itself progressively stripped of functions and influence.

The Covenant and the Joint Conference

The Report calls for the Parliament and the councils to commit themselves to a concordat or covenant, setting out the basis of their working relationship, and to set up a standing Joint Conference where MSPs and council representatives can hold a dialogue on the basis of equality.[13] A draft Covenant is included as an appendix to the Report containing the following general principles:

- respect for each other's roles;
- partnership on strategic issues;
- genuine consultation prior to any major restructuring of local government;
- pre-legislative discussion on local government issues;
- a sound financial base for local government;
- the principle of subsidiarity;
- openness and accountability;
- a recognition of councils' key roles in service provision and as co-ordinators of service delivery.

The Covenant should not be enforced through the courts nor by any other formal mechanism but by the political necessity of keeping to it. However, the Joint Conference should monitor its application and consider modifications from time to time.

It is suggested that the Joint Conference should consist of not more than 15 representatives each of the Parliament (not Ministers) and of local government. The chairmanship [sic] should alternate annually between the parliamentary and the local government sides. It should meet regularly and local government policy issues should be able to be placed on the agenda by either side. Any local authority or MSP should have the right to submit papers on agenda items. Scottish Ministers may be invited and should be entitled to attend and speak. At least once a year all council leaders should be invited to attend. The Conference should work towards improved public service standards, provide an opportunity for the exchange of ideas, review policy and consider legislative proposals. It should produce an annual "State of Local Government" report.

Relations between local government and the Scottish Ministers

There was already in existence, prior to the establishment of the Parliament, a formal working agreement between the Convention of Scottish Local Authorities (COSLA) and the Scottish Office. McIntosh recommends that a similar agreement should be established between local government and the Scottish Ministers.[14] A draft is included as an appendix to the Report. The general principles are almost identical to those suggested for the Covenant. In addition, it suggests that the Scottish Ministers should commit themselves to consultation with COSLA, as the representative body of local authorities in Scotland, on policy issues affecting local government. COSLA should also be consulted during the pre-legislative phase on legislative proposals affecting local government. Sufficient time should be allowed, where possible, for a considered and representative response.

Scottish Ministers should always convey public announcements

---

[13]The McIntosh Report, para. 34.
[14]The McIntosh Report, para. 45.

directly concerning local government to COSLA no later than to the media and, where possible, in advance. COSLA should reciprocate in relation to announcements concerning Scottish Ministers.

The First Minister and the Scottish Ministers responsible for major services should meet COSLA on a regular basis to exchange views. Either side should be able to request *ad hoc* meetings to discuss a specific subject. COSLA should be consulted on the appointment of local government representatives to other bodies.

A power of general competence

The legal position at the moment is that local authorities may do only those things which statute law empowers them to do. Anything else is *ultra vires*. In many other countries local government may do anything for the benefit of their communities which is not specifically reserved or prohibited or provided for through other legislation. Such a power is generally referred to as a power of general competence.

The McIntosh Report recognises that legislation giving local government a power of general competence would require careful drafting but nevertheless sees significant benefits in providing such a power and recommends that such a statutory power should be introduced. The benefits of such a power include:

- giving specific statutory form to the principle of subsidiarity on a parallel with the Scotland Act itself which empowers the Scottish Parliament to do whatever is not specifically reserved to Westminster;
- giving statutory expression to the unwritten purpose of a local council, namely to be the voice of its people and promote their interests;
- facilitating the process of community planning by increasing the freedom of councils to take part in joint action with other agencies.

There is no doubt that the *ultra vires* rule has caused problems to local government and to those with whom it works. For example, it was decided in *Morgan Guaranty Trust Company of New York* v. *Lothian Regional Council*[15] that local authorities had no power to engage in interest rate swaps, a decision which, along with similar English decisions, led to unwillingness on the part of financial institutions to deal with local authorities. Local government would therefore welcome a power of general competence embodied in statute.

The Response of the Scottish Executive

The initial response was made by the Minister for Communities in the Scottish Parliament within a few days of the publication of the McIntosh Report. She announced that a Leadership Forum would be

---

[15] 1995 SCLR 225; 1995 SLT 215.

established to bring together Scottish Ministers and the Leaders of the 32 councils. The first meeting was held in September 1999.

She also announced that the Parliament's Local Government Committee would lead public debate on various issues, including the proposed Covenant and the Joint Conference.

A consultation paper was issued by the Scottish Executive in the autumn of 1999. It made no mention of the Covenant or the Joint Conference but announced that there would be further consultation on a range of issues, including a power of general competence and on the allocation of local government finance within the current policy framework.

FUTURE PROSPECTS FOR LOCAL GOVERNMENT

The Report of the McIntosh Commission raises very contentious issues relating to the internal management of local authorities, the electoral cycle, the voting system and others which are outside the remit of this book. These are the issues in which the Scottish Executive has shown the greatest interest and it appears that local government is to undergo another period of upheaval. The Scottish Parliament has the power to legislate on virtually every aspect of local government and part of the coalition agreement between the Labour Party and the Liberal Democrats refers to the Liberal Democrats' commitment to the introduction of proportional representation for elections to local government. It is likely, therefore, that the Scottish Executive will introduce legislation on the electoral system and other issues relating to local government within the first two years of its existence. It announced its intention to pass a Bill to regulate ethical standards in public life within the first year and a draft Bill was published in November 1999.[16] As far as the public are concerned, the services delivered by local government affect them, literally from the cradle (registration of births) to the grave (cemeteries and crematoria provision). Most Scots are educated in local authority schools, and many live in council houses. Leisure facilities, roads, refuse collection and disposal and many other services impinge on the life of every citizen. What is important to the public is the efficient and effective delivery of these services and value for the money they pay in council tax. What is also important is the local dimension. The delivery of services should take account of local needs. That is one reason why local government exists.

The old relationship between local government and the Scottish Office has changed with the establishment of a Scottish Parliament and a Scottish Government. A significant element in the character of the new relationship is the number of MSPs who have a background in local government. It is important that the relationship between the

---

[16]The Ethical Standards in Public Life etc. (Scotland) Bill. This Bill also contained the very controversial proposal to repeal section 2A of the Local Government Act 1986 which is better (though mistakenly) known as section 28. This section prohibits local authorities from promoting homosexuality.

two elected institutions is not one of rivalry, but of co-operation. The public will not be particularly interested in squabbles between the two, but they may become disenchanted with both if the results are less satisfactory services. A covenant as suggested by McIntosh, adopted early in the life of the Parliament, may well put the relationship on a stable footing, but it will require good will on both sides. Only time will tell if local government will survive in its present form and with its present range of responsibilities.

THE SCOTTISH PARLIAMENT AND OTHER PUBLIC BODIES

Despite the wide range of services delivered by local government, there is a huge range of public services which are delivered by unelected public bodies. Most of these are officially called Non-Departmental Public Bodies (NDPBs), but they are popularly known as quangos. They take a number of different forms. Some are advisory (such as the Health Appointments Advisory Committee), some have judicial functions (such as tribunals and the Children's Panels), some are regulatory (such as the Scottish Environmental Protection Agency) while others have executive functions and control large budgets (such as Scottish Homes, Scottish Enterprise and the Water Authorities). Their members have been appointed by the Secretary of State for Scotland or, since July 1999, by the Scottish Ministers and there is no statutory requirement for any councillors to be appointed. There have been many criticisms of NDPBs, not the least of which is the lack of direct accountability to the public. In the White Paper, *Scotland's Parliament*, the Government expressed concern at the extent to which vital public services are run by unelected bodies.[17] Responsibility for all Scottish public bodies whose remits run wholly within devolved areas passed to the Scottish Parliament and Executive under the rules governing the Parliament's legislative competence which have been dealt with above.[18] As with local government, the Parliament is able to wind them up, alter their remits or merge some of them together. The Scottish Executive has taken over from the Secretary of State the powers to make appointments to their boards, to fund them and generally direct their activities. There are 38 executive NDPBs and 56 advisory bodies and tribunals. Almost 3,600 persons are appointed to these (three times the number of elected councillors). They spend just under £2bn a year, while NHS health boards and trusts, which are not NDPBs but which are generally considered to be quangos and which have almost 350 appointed members, spend £4.5bn a year. The most up-to-date list of such bodies is set out in Annex A to the Scottish Executive's consultation paper on appointments to public bodies, issued in February 2000.[19] It includes NDPBs (including Scottish Enterprise, the Crofters Commission, the National

---

[17]Para 6.7.
[18]See Chapter 2 above.
[19]*Appointments to Public Bodies in Scotland: Modernising the System, Consultation Paper*. The Scottish Executive, February 2000.

Galleries and the National Library of Scotland and many others); advisory bodies (including the Scottish Law Commission, the Scottish Advisory Committee on Drug Misuse and the Historic Buildings Council for Scotland); three nationalised industries (the Scottish Transport Group, Highlands and Islands Airports Ltd, and Caledonian MacBrayne Ltd); tribunals (including Children's Panels and the Horse Racing Betting Levy Appeal Tribunal for Scotland); public corporations (the three water authorities) and health bodies (including health boards and NHS trusts).

FUTURE PROSPECTS FOR PUBLIC BODIES

Given the unique role of local government which stems from its elected status, the McIntosh Commission recommended that in any review of other bodies delivering public services, the option of transfer to local government should always be considered. Likewise where new services are being developed prior consideration should always be given to whether local government should be the vehicle of delivery, subject to efficiency and cost-effectiveness.[20]

The initial response of the Scottish Executive to McIntosh's recommendations was to confirm that whenever a periodic review of a quango is carried out, the option of the transfer of its functions to local government would be considered as one of the options.

In December 1999, it was announced that Scottish Homes would come under the direct control of the Scottish Ministers as a government agency. In February 2000, the Finance Minister announced a major consultation exercise on the appointment of members to quangos. The key objectives of the procedures for making public appointments system are[21]:

- to ensure public confidence in the appointment process by making it fair, open and transparent with appointments being made on merit;
- to be proportionate, that is appropriate to the nature of the posts and the weight of their responsibilities;
- to provide clarity and structure;
- to secure quality outcomes;
- to encourage a wider range of people to apply for public appointments;
- to be accessible and informative.

The Scottish Executive also wish to increase the number of women and people from an ethnic minority background on public bodies. It is also possible that a Scottish Commissioner for Public Appointments will be appointed to monitor, regulate and provide advice on

---

[20]The McIntosh Report, para. 62.
[21]*Appointments to Public Bodies in Scotland: Modernising the System, Consultation Paper.* The Scottish Executive, Chapter 2.

departmental procedures and deal with complaints.[22] The Parliament itself might also have a role both at the pre-appointment stage and in post-appointment scrutiny.[23]

In addition, the Ethical Standards in Public Life etc. (Scotland) Bill proposes a model code of conduct for members of various devolved public bodies and the establishment of a Standards Commission which would have the power to censure, suspend or remove from office a member who breaches the code.

CROSS-BORDER PUBLIC AUTHORITIES

Certain public bodies have remits which cover matters some of which are within the legislative competence of the Parliament and others outwith it. Such bodies include the British Wool Marketing Board, the Sports Council, the Advisory Committee on Hazardous Substances, the UK Live Transplant Support Service Authority, the British Tourist Authority and many others. These are known as cross-border authorities.[24] Scottish Ministers have the right to be consulted by their UK counterparts on the appointment of members and officers and on any specific function whose exercise might affect Scotland. The Scotland Act also makes it possible for the exercise of certain functions of cross-border public bodies to be transferred from UK Ministers to Scottish Ministers.[25] It is also possible for the Scottish Parliament to set up separate Scottish bodies to handle the specifically Scottish and devolved aspects of the cross-border authorities' work.

Some public bodies deal solely with matters which are reserved to the UK Parliament. These include the Equal Opportunities Commission, the Commission for Racial Equality, the BBC, the Post Office and the Benefits Agency. Although they deal with matters which are reserved, their activities continue to be of great interest to Scots. The Scottish Parliament's Standing Orders enable committees to invite the submission of reports and the presentation of oral evidence[26] to its committees. In certain cases, the Scottish Executive may be consulted prior to the appointment of chairmen or governors.

---

[22]*Appointments to Public Bodies in Scotland: Modernising the System, Consultation Paper.* The Scottish Executive, Chapter 6.

[23]*Appointments to Public Bodies in Scotland: Modernising the System, Consultation Paper.* The Scottish Executive, Chapter 7.

[24]Section 88.

[25]Section 89.

[26]The Standing Orders of the Scottish Parliament, Rule 12.4.

10. THE SCOTTISH PARLIAMENT AND EUROPE

INTRODUCTION

Scotland, of course, is not just a part of the United Kingdom, but part of Europe. The issue of how the establishment of a Scottish Parliament would affect relationships with European institutions, and the European Union in particular, is one that was considered in the final report of the Scottish Constitutional Convention, and the government made various proposals regarding the relationship with the European Union in the White Paper, *Scotland's Parliament*.[1]

The issue is important because the European Communities can and do make legislation which will be binding in all Member States, or which Member States are obliged to implement. If a Member State has devolved certain of its powers to a devolved legislature (such as the Parliament), a mechanism has to be put in place to ensure that such a devolved legislature both implements European legislation which the Member State is obliged to implement and also does not seek to make legislation which would contravene existing European law. Such a mechanism is important not least because the Member State could in the last analysis be fined by the European Court of Justice, or be required to pay compensation to anyone whose interests had been damaged by a failure of a devolved legislature to comply with European law.

The reverse side of the coin is that it is only the Member States that participate in the Council of Ministers which plays the most important part in the legislative process of the European Communities (the only possible mechanism for formal participation in that legislative activity being through the minimal consultative rights given to regions in the Committee of the Regions). As a result, a devolved legislature will find itself being required to implement European legislation in the adoption of which it has had no say. It can readily be seen that such a situation, although perfectly feasible in terms of constitutional arrangements, is one that might present political difficulties both for the devolved legislature and the sovereign legislature of the state concerned.

The questions to be addressed in the devolution scheme for Scotland, therefore, were these. First, what mechanism should be put in place to ensure that the Scottish Parliament complied with European legislation and other obligations where these concerned devolved matters. Second, how could the Scottish Parliament be given some role in the European legislative and policy making

---

[1] Chapter 5.

process, even though it is the UK which, as the Member State, is the entity which has the right to take part in that process.

THE LEGISLATIVE PROVISIONS

The Scotland Act seeks to ensure that the Parliament does not breach the UK's European obligations by a few simple mechanisms:

First, it provides that any Act of the Scottish Parliament which is incompatible with the "Convention rights" enshrined in UK law by the Human Rights Act 1998, or with EC law is outside the legislative competence of the Parliament, and does not become law.[2]

Second, it provides that a member of the Scottish Executive cannot make any subordinate legislation, or do anything else, which is incompatible with the Convention rights or with EC law (subject to a reservation in respect of certain acts by the Lord Advocate relating to the prosecution of crime).[3]

Third, UK Ministers will continue to be able to implement EC obligations by means of secondary legislation, even where it covers matters which are devolved to the Scottish Parliament.[4]

Fourth, the UK Parliament retains a general right to legislate for Scotland, even over devolved matters, and clearly this power could be used to ensure compliance by the Scottish Executive and Parliament with the UK's obligations under EC law.

Moreover, in the White Paper, *Scotland's Parliament*,[5] it was envisaged that there might be cases where (with the agreement of the Scottish Executive) implementation of EU obligations affecting devolved matters might be achieved by UK (or GB) legislation rather than specifically Scottish legislation. Furthermore, where EU obligations are to be implemented by separate legislation in the Scottish Parliament, it is stated that "there will be arrangements with the UK Government to ensure that differences of approach are compatible with the need for consistency of effect, and to avoid the risk of financial penalties falling on the UK." It can be presumed, therefore, if any concerns arising from such differences of approach cannot be resolved by agreement between the UK Government and the Scottish Executive, the UK Government may well use its reserved powers to legislate on devolved matters to resolve the dispute as it sees fit.

Accordingly, the legislation contains mechanisms to deal with any eventuality that might arise if the Scottish Parliament or Executive fails to comply with obligations under European law. An attempt to pass legislation or do anything which conflicts with such obligations is unlawful. If the Scottish Parliament or Executive refuses to legislate

---

[2] Section 29.

[3] Section 57(2).

[4] Section 57(1). The power of UK Ministers to implement Community obligations by subordinate legislation is given by section 2(2) of the European Communities Act 1972. See also Schedule 5, para 7.

[5] Para 5.8.

to take account of changing European obligations and as a result by an act of omission places itself in contravention of such obligations, the UK Government can enforce compliance by passing both primary and secondary legislation in appropriate terms. In addition, of course, the allocation of block grant is a matter entirely for the UK government and Parliament, so no doubt any financial penalty falling on the UK as a result of such a breach of obligation could be compensated by a commensurate reduction in the grant paid to the Scottish Executive. (Furthermore, the Concordat on EU policy issues, which is considered in the following section, commits the Scottish Executive to meeting the costs of any financial penalties imposed on the United Kingdom as a result of a failure on the part of the Scottish administration to implement EU obligations in devolved matters.)

CONSULTATIVE ARRANGEMENTS

The requirement of the devolved Parliament and Executive to comply with European obligations is therefore clearly a cornerstone of the Act. However, the Scottish Parliament and Executive are not given any statutory rights in the Act to participate in the decision-making process that eventually results in European legislation. This is in contrast with some other European countries, where devolved or federal regions and states have, in some cases, been given a legal right to take part, to some degree at least, in the process whereby their Member State takes part in the European decision-making and legislative process.[6]

Instead, the UK Government proposed that a number of consultative, but non-statutory, methods should be established to allow the Scottish Parliament and Executive to play a part in those aspects of European business which affect devolved areas. This statement of intent was put into effect in one of the concordats agreed between the UK Government and the various devolved administrations after their establishment.[7] The *Concordat on Co-ordination of European Union Policy Issues*[8] states that it is the UK Government's wish to involve the Scottish Executive as directly and fully as possible in decision-making on EU matters which touch on devolved areas (including non-devolved matters which would have an important impact on Scotland). It emphasises that such involvement by the Scottish Executive would be subject to "mutual respect for the confidentiality of discussions and adherence by the Scottish Executive to the resulting UK line". It indicates that without such respect and adherence it would be impossible to maintain such close working relationships, presumably implying that a Scottish Executive which refused to be bound by such conditions would be at risk of losing its right to participate in decision-making on EU matters.

---

[6]For example, Germany and Belgium.
[7]See Chapter 7 for further details of the concordats.
[8]The text of the concordat was published in Cm 4444 and can be found at http://www.scotland.gov.uk/memorandum. See p 86.

The mechanisms established to ensure such participation include the following:

- a commitment by the UK Government to provide the Scottish Executive with full and comprehensive information, as early as possible, on all business within the EU which appears likely to be of interest to it, with a reciprocal requirement on the Scottish Executive to provide information to the UK Government on such issues in its turn;
- access by officials of the Scottish Executive to the same relevant papers on EU issues as their Whitehall counterparts;
- reference of matters to the Joint Ministerial Committee[9] for discussion where differences between the Scottish and UK Governments cannot be resolved by more informal contact;
- the possibility of Ministers from the Scottish Executive attending meetings of the Council of Ministers on relevant matters, although it would be up to the relevant UK Minister to decide whether or not such attendance was appropriate. In certain cases, the Scottish Minister could speak for the United Kingdom as a whole, although the UK "lead minister" will retain overall responsibility for negotiations (similar arrangements would apply to allow participation in EU meetings at official level);
- the right of the Scottish Executive to establish an office in Brussels, for the purpose of assisting direct relationships with other European regional governments and with the institutions of the European Communities. Such an office is restricted, however, to dealing with matters which are within the competence of the Scottish Parliament and Executive, and is required to work closely with, and in a complementary manner to, the UK representation in Brussels. This qualification is clearly intended to prevent such an office turning into a "Scottish embassy" or something similar, as advocated from time to time by the SNP. The Scottish Executive established such a European office very soon after devolution, in October 1999, sharing *Scotland House* with *Scotland Europa*, an umbrella body representing public, private, and voluntary sector interests, which had already operated a Brussels office for a number of years.
- the delegation to the Scottish Executive of the appointment of the Scottish members of the UK representation on the Committee of the Regions, and the Economic and Social Committee;
- a commitment that the relevant Whitehall department would keep the Scottish Executive informed of EU legislative proposals, in order that the Scottish Parliament can, if it wishes, scrutinise such matters, and let the UK Government have its views on such proposals;

---

[9]See p 85.

- detailed arrangements for ensuring that new EU obligations are implemented in Scotland as and when they arise, and for the co-ordination of the UK response to any proceedings taken against the United Kingdom for alleged breach of an EU obligation concerned a devolved matter.

It was emphasised in the White Paper *Scotland's Parliament* that the guiding principle on European issues is that there should be "the closest possible working relationships and involvement" between the Scottish and UK layers of government, requiring the Scottish Executive to work in a "spirit of collaboration and trust" with the UK Government.[10] Similar sentiments are expressed in the concordat on EU policy issues. At the end of the day, however, the concordat is not legally binding, but as with all the other concordats, is intended to be "binding in honour only". Underpinning these statements of intent is a firm statutory framework to ensure that at the end of the day Scotland complies with EC obligations, either by the action of the Scottish Parliament and Executive, or failing which, by the UK Government and Parliament taking steps to ensure compliance.

DEALING WITH EUROPEAN ISSUES

Nevertheless, if the statements of intent outlined above are reflected in the actual relations between the UK and Scottish levels of government, it is clear that the Scottish Parliament and Executive will each have a real role to play in the development of UK policy on Europe so far as it affects devolved matters. Given its legislative powers, the Scottish Parliament will be able to decide how EC legislation is implemented in devolved matters (except in the unusual case of being overruled by the UK Parliament's reserved power of legislation), and the Parliament has decided to take the opportunity offered to it of scrutinising EU legislative proposals in advance. To deal with such matters, the Parliament's European Committee has been given a remit to deal both with specific items of EU legislation, and wider EU issues as well. It therefore has the ability, if it wishes, to fulfil both the specialist function of scrutinising EU legislation, and also the role of a generalist committee on European affairs. The CSG saw the European committee as playing an important role in the new Parliament, and suggested that, as well as its work within Scotland, it could also develop close links with similar committees at Westminster and the Assemblies in Northern Ireland and Wales. Such links have begun to be developed, particularly between the officials of the various bodies. It was further suggested that the European committee should build close links with Members of the European Parliament from Scotland, and that it could also invite the European Commission to give evidence. The committee has also established informal links with similar committees in a number of other European regional assemblies. It appears, therefore, to be developing an interest both in wider

---

[10]Para 5.12.

European issues and contacts as well as specific European legislation, very much as suggested by the CSG.

It should be noted, however, that the CSG report suggested that the European Committee might wish to refer matters as appropriate to other committees or to the full Parliament, and the committee now established will refer matters in such a way from time to time. CSG thought that much of the implementation of European legislation would fall to individual "subject" committees of the Parliament, although it expected that the European Committee would take an overview of the process. In addition, an important role in the process of implementing EU legislation will fall upon the Subordinate Legislation Committee, as subordinate legislation made by members of the Scottish Executive will often be the mechanism by which such legislation is put into effect in Scotland. It is likely, therefore, that the long-term role of the European Committee in implementing European legislation will only become once the Parliament has been in operation for some time. Its effectiveness will no doubt depend, to some extent, on how the non-statutory arrangements set out in the relevant concordat are put into practice by the Scottish Executive and Parliament.

CONVENTION RIGHTS

As has been mentioned, the Scotland Act includes measures not only to ensure compliance with EC law, but also with "Convention rights". These are the rights laid down in the European Convention on Human Rights (ECHR), which the Human Rights Act 1998 has for the first time enshrined in UK law. Reference should be made to the Act for the full extent of these new rights, but there are many devolved matters where it is easy to see how the Convention rights may have major implications both for the Parliament and the Executive. (As mentioned above, the Human Rights Act is one of the Acts of the UK Parliament which the Scottish Parliament is specifically prohibited from modifying).[11]

For example, the criminal and civil legal systems of Scotland will have to be consistent with *the right to liberty and security* and *the right to a fair trial*, and will have to ensure that there is *no punishment without law* (which last provision prohibits, in general, retrospective legislation). Social policy will have to comply with *the right to respect for private and family life*. Scotland already has experience of parents turning to the ECHR to vindicate their *right to education in conformity with their own religious and philosophical convictions*. Land reform will have to respect the convention rights relating to the *protection of property*. This list of illustrative examples by no means exhausts the list of possible implications of the new Convention rights[12] for

---

[11]Schedule 4, para 1. See Chapter 2 above.
[12]Schedule 1 to the Human Rights Act 1998 lists the "Convention rights" enshrined by that Act.

legislation by the Parliament and government activity by the Scottish Administration.

As legislation by the Parliament will be outside its competence if it is incompatible with Convention rights, the existence of such rights can give rise to challenges to its legislation both prior to Royal Assent, and thereafter. Similar challenges can be made to actions of the Scottish Administration if they are incompatible with Convention rights. As discussed above,[13] the Convention rights were brought into effect for devolved matters in advance of their general implementation within the United Kingdom under the Human Rights Act. By the end of 1999 there had been a large number of legal challenges made to actions of the Scottish Administration, most, if not all, relating to the actions of the prosecution authorities, and usually relying on a claim that the Convention right to a fair trial[14] had been breached.

The Human Rights Act also makes it unlawful for a public authority "to act in a way which is incompatible with a Convention right",[15] unless the act in question is, in essence, based upon valid primary or subordinate legislation. (An Act of the Scottish Parliament will not be valid if it infringes Convention rights). It seems clear that under the Human Rights Act, the Scottish Executive would be regarded as such a public authority, and under a strict construction of that Act, the Scottish Parliament itself would probably also be considered a public authority (as it is only the Houses of the Westminster Parliament that are expressly excluded from the definition of "public authority"[16]). Any such unlawful actions by public authorities can be struck down by the courts, which can also award damages to the person who has suffered as a result.[17]

---

[13]See Chapter 7.

[14]An early example of a successful challenge can be seen in *Starrs & Chalmers* v. *Ruxton* 2000 SLT 42, in which the court held that a trial presided over by a temporary sheriff, whose tenure ultimately depended on the same person as the prosecutor, was not an independent and impartial tribunal. This challenge had major effects on the role that temporary sheriffs were able to play in criminal matters.

[15]Human Rights Act 1998, s. 6(1).

[16]Section 6(3).

[17]Section 8.

11. RESHAPING BRITAIN

The rioting in the streets of Glasgow and Edinburgh which greeted the announcement of the terms of the Treaty of Union in 1706 was not exactly followed by dancing in the streets on the passing of the Scotland Act on 19th November 1998. Nevertheless, the Scots had turned out in considerable numbers to vote "Yes/Yes" in the two-question referendum in September 1997[1] and the turn-out for the first elections on 6th May 1999 was a respectable 59%. It is probable that most Scots see the establishment of the Scottish Parliament as a constitutional landmark in isolation — the restoration of the old Scots Parliament which was abolished almost 300 years ago, albeit with reduced powers.

In the months immediately preceding the election in May, it became increasingly clear that policy pronouncements from Westminster and Downing Street were excluding Scotland. The Queen's speech on the opening of the 1998/9 Parliamentary session in November 1998 included no Scottish measure of any significance. Scottish policy-making is largely to be left to the Scottish Parliament which has legislative competence over a very wide range of areas. This is generally welcomed by the Scottish people many of whom resented the way in which the Conservative governments of 1979–97 imposed policies on Scotland for which the Scots had not voted. All the political parties in Scotland now accept the fact of devolution to Scotland, even the Conservative Party which had steadfastly opposed it under the premierships of Margaret Thatcher and John Major. The Scottish National Party accepts devolution in the short-term while not relinquishing its long-term goal of independence.

Devolution to Scotland should be seen, however, not in isolation, but as part of the new government's deliberate policy of decentralisation of government and as part of a wide-ranging programme of constitutional reform which will have major repercussions for the way in which the UK is governed.

DECENTRALISATION OF GOVERNMENT

The government's programme of decentralisation extends to the whole of the UK, not just to Scotland. The Government of Wales Act 1998 established a directly-elected National Assembly for Wales which assumed most of the responsibilities of the Secretary of State

---

[1]The turn-out in the referendum was 60 per cent, not as high as in general election turn-out which usually exceeds 70 per cent, but much higher than the normal turn-out for local elections which rarely reaches 50 per cent.

for Wales.[2] Unlike the Scottish Parliament, the Assembly does not have legislative powers. Its powers are administrative only, but there is a statutory duty placed on the Secretary of State for Wales to consult the Assembly on the government's legislative programme for Wales.[3] The Welsh Executive and the various subject committees do, however, have the power to prepare secondary legislation for submission to the Assembly for debate and approval.[4]

In the case of Northern Ireland, the Northern Ireland Act 1998 established (albeit rather precariously) a Northern Ireland Assembly. This Assembly has legislative and administrative powers. Like the Scotland Act 1998, the Northern Ireland Act 1998 adopts the retaining model for the distribution of legislative powers. In the case of Northern Ireland, however, in addition to matters reserved to the UK Parliament,[5] there are matters which are excepted from the Assembly's legislative competence.[6] Because of the religious and political circumstances of Northern Ireland, there are special provisions to ensure cross-community[7] support for various measures such as the appointment of the First Minister and deputy First Minister.

A Council of the Isles has been established and renamed the British-Irish Council. This is comprised of representatives of the British and Irish Governments, the Scottish Parliament, the National Assembly for Wales, the Northern Ireland Assembly and the representatives of the Isle of Man and the Channel Islands.[8] The council meets at summit level twice a year and on other occasions when appropriate. Its members exchange information, discuss, consult and endeavour to reach agreement on co-operation on matters of mutual interest within the competence of the relevant Parliaments and Assemblies. The elected institutions will be encouraged to develop inter-parliamentary links. Other institutions established by the Northern Ireland Act 1998 are the North-South Ministerial Council and the British Irish Intergovernmental Conference.[9] Another major constitutional development is the Disqualifications Bill the provisions of which will allow members of the legislature of the Republic of Ireland to sit in the House of Commons and in the Northern Ireland Assembly.

England has not escaped the government's decentralising zeal. The

---

[2] Government of Wales Act 1998, s. 22 and Schedule 3.

[3] Ibid section 31.

[4] Ibid section 22.

[5] Northern Ireland Act 1998, Schedule 3.

[6] Ibid Schedule 2.

[7] Cross-community support requires set percentages of designated Unionists and designated Nationalists to vote in favour of an issue.

[8] The Belfast Agreement, Strand 3.

[9] Unfortunately, because of major disagreements between the Unionists and the Nationalists over the decommissioning of arms, the government had to rush onto the statute book in February 2000 the Northern Ireland Act 2000 which gives the UK Government the power to suspend the Northern Ireland Assembly, the British-Irish Council, the North-South Ministerial Council and the British-Irish Intergovernmental Conference. The Secretary of State for Northern Ireland used the powers in this Act to suspend these institutions on 11th February 2000. The suspension will cease only when the Secretary of State for Northern Ireland makes a restoration order.

Regional Development Agencies Act 1998 established nine regional agencies in England, all of which, with the exception of London, were operational by 1999. They have powers to further the economic development and regeneration of their areas, and promote business efficiency and employment in both urban and rural areas.[10] These agencies are quangos, their members being appointed by a Government Minister, not directly elected.

In London, the government has established an elected Greater London Authority with a directly elected mayor and Assembly.[11] The Greater London Authority does not have its own tax-raising powers but raises revenue from precepts, road tolls and parking fees. The Mayor runs new transport and economic development bodies and has responsibility for attracting new investment, job creation and the regeneration of rundown urban areas. These are managed by the London Development Agency.

The constitutional developments in Scotland, Wales and Northern Ireland have acted as a stimulus for debate in England and in time the English regions may come to demand elected regional assemblies similar to the Greater London Authority or the National Assembly for Wales. If the English regions' demands were to go further and they aspired to assemblies or parliaments with legislative powers like those in Scotland and Northern Ireland, the UK might be set on a course which would lead to federalism. Certainly, in those circumstances, the role of the UK Parliament would have to be redefined.

CONSTITUTIONAL REFORM

The Labour government's programme of devolution and decentralisation has to be set in a wider context of constitutional reform much of which was set out in its manifesto for the 1997 General Election.

The European Convention on Human Rights has been incorporated into UK law by the Human Rights Act 1998, improving the access of UK citizens to the rights and freedoms guaranteed by the Convention. The Government published its Freedom of Information Bill in 1999.

In January 1999, the Government issued a White Paper, *Modernising Parliament: Reforming the House of Lords*.[12] The first step was to legislate for the removal of the right of hereditary peers to sit and vote in the House of Lords. Before the year was out legislation was on the statute book.[13] There is now a transitional house in which 92 hereditary peers sit on a temporary basis along with the life peers. There is a proposal for an independent, non-statutory Appointments Commission which is responsible for identifying suitable Cross Bench[14] nominees and for vetting all the political parties' nominations. The government also established a Royal Commission, under the chairmanship of Lord

---

[10]Regional Development Agencies Act 1998, s. 4.
[11]Greater London Authority Act 1999.
[12]Cm. 4183.
[13]House of Lords Act 1999.
[14]Cross Bench peers are peers who do not belong to any political party.

Wakeham, to consider and make recommendations on the role and functions of a second chamber and the methods of its composition. The Royal Commission reported in January 2000.[15] Its preference, in terms of composition, was for a chamber consisting of mainly appointed members with a small number of regional elected members. The government has yet to decide as to how to take further reform of the House of Lords forward.

Even the monarchy is considering how to modernise itself. The rules which govern succession to the Crown mean that male heirs and their children (regardless of sex) take precedence over female heirs, while the Act of Settlement 1700 and the Acts of Union 1706–7 confined succession to members of the Protestant religion and specifically excludes Roman Catholics and those married to Roman Catholics. These rules seem increasingly out of date in modern Britain and may well be abolished before long. The Scottish Parliament has unanimously passed a resolution calling for the repeal of that part of the Act of Settlement which excludes Roman Catholics and those married to Roman Catholics from succession to the throne, but the UK government has not as yet found the legislative time to do this.[16]

Changes to the franchise are under way to increase the turnout at election. The Representation of the People Act 2000 aims to make it easier for certain people to register and to vote and allows for pilot projects of innovative electoral procedures in local government elections in England and Wales. Political parties, which have been almost invisible in statute until now, have to be registered under the Registration of Political Parties Act 1998[17] and there are to be restrictions on the sources of donations to prohibit foreign and anonymous donors. Restrictions are also to be placed on the amount of money a political party can spend in an election campaign and on the amount spent by individuals or organisations in support of or in opposition to political parties. In addition, shareholder consent will have to be obtained before a company can make a donation to a political party or incur political expenditure.[18] Reform of the voting system is also under way. The Scottish Parliament and the National Assembly for Wales were elected by the mixture of the first past the post and party list systems known as the additional member system.[19] The members of the Northern Ireland Assembly were elected under the system known as the single transferable vote. The members of the Greater London Authority and the Mayor were elected under a system called the supplementary vote, while the elections to the European Parliament in

[15]*A House for the Future:* The Report of the Royal Commission on the Reform of the House of Lords. Cm. 4534.

[16]The process of reforming the law relating to the succession to the Crown is complex and legislating to change it would be a lengthy process involving the amendment not only of various UK statutes, including the Acts of Union, but also the statutes of 15 Commonwealth countries of which the Queen is Head of State. The Government has stated that repeal does not come high in its present list of priorities.

[17]See Chapter 3.

[18]Political Parties, Elections and Referendums Bill.

[19]See Chapter 3.

1999 were on the party list system. All of these, to a greater or lesser degree, produce results in which the number of seats won by each political party is proportional to the number of votes cast for that party. They reduce the likelihood of one party winning an outright majority and thus coalition and inter-party co-operation becomes more likely.

The replacement of the first past the post system for elections to the UK Parliament could have wide repercussions for the way the country is governed. In December 1997, the Government established the Independent Commission on the Voting System, chaired by Lord Jenkins of Hillhead. The Commission reported in October 1998[20] and recommended that the best alternative to the first past the post system would be a mixed system under which 80 to 85 per cent of MPs would be elected on an individual constituency basis, using a system known as the Alternative Vote, with the remainder being elected on a list system.[21] It remains to be seen what the government will recommend, but a referendum on the issue has been promised by the Prime Minister.

At the end of 1999 the Government introduced a Bill to ensure the fair conduct of referendums which will provide for grants of up to £600,000 to campaign bodies, free mailing of referendum addresses and free air time for referendum campaign broadcasts. It will also place restrictions on the publication and distribution of promotional material by central and local government and on referendum campaign expenditure by political parties.[22]

Until recently, referenda were used very sparingly by UK governments. In 1973, a referendum was held in Northern Ireland on the question of continued union with the UK. In 1975, there was a referendum on the question of the UK's continued membership of the European Communities. The implementation of the Scotland and Wales Acts 1978 was put to the people of Scotland and of Wales in 1979.

Since the Labour Government came to power in May 1997, there were as many referenda in less than two years as there had been in the previous 25. In 1997 the people of Scotland were consulted on the establishment of the Scottish Parliament and, separately, on the question of that Parliament having tax-varying powers.[23] In the same year the Welsh were consulted on the establishment of the National Assembly for Wales. In 1998, the citizens of London were consulted on the question of a directly-elected mayor and an elected Greater London Authority, and the people of Northern Ireland were asked to vote on the Belfast Agreement. (The people of the Republic of Ireland were consulted in a referendum on the same issue by the Irish Government.) The government is committed to further referenda on electoral reform, as mentioned above, on a single European currency,

---

[20] Cm. 4090–1.

[21] Ibid ch. 9.

[22] Political Parties, Elections and Referendums Bill / Act 2000.

[23] See Chapter 1.

in relation to devolution to the English regions and on other constitutional issues.

As a result of the doctrine of parliamentary sovereignty,[24] referenda are advisory only and cannot be considered as legally binding on the Government or Parliament. Nevertheless, the Government has regarded the results of the referenda held so far to be morally binding and a mandate for the actions they propose to take. Certainly the Scotland Act 1998 had an easier passage through Parliament, in particular through the House of Lords, as a result of the overwhelming support for the Scottish Parliament expressed by the Scottish people in the referendum in 1997. As the British become more used to being consulted by government on major issues, there could, in the longer-term, be implications for the sovereignty of parliament.

There is no doubt that for those who are interested in the constitution, these are exciting times. The establishment of the Scottish Parliament in 1999 has led, almost immediately, to major differences in the way Scotland is governed. The question of independence for Scotland at some time in the future will not go away. The SNP are committed to holding a referendum on the issue during the first term of a Scottish Parliament, in which they win control.

For the rest of the UK, government is changing in ways that would not have been contemplated less than a decade ago. The constitutional map of the UK may look very different in the not too distant future and the "Mother of Parliaments" may discover that her children want to abandon her.

---

[24]See Chapter 2.

GLOSSARY OF TERMS

Absolute majority: a number of votes which is equivalent to more than half of the total number of seats in the Parliament. The figure in a Parliament with 129 seats is 65 or more.

Advocate General: the Advocate General (for Scotland) is a Law Officer whose task is to advise the UK Government on matters of law relating to Scottish devolution.

Committee Bill: a Bill proposed by a Committee of the Scottish Parliament (rather than the Scottish Executive or an individual MSP).

Community law: the law of the European Communities, *i.e.* all the rights, powers, liabilities, obligations and restrictions from time to time created or arising under the European Community Treaties and all remedies and procedures provided by these treaties.

Constituency members: members of the Scottish Parliament who are returned by the first past the post method of election and who represent an individual constituency. In the first Scottish Parliament there are 73 constituency members.

Consultative Steering Group (CSG): a group which contained representatives of the main political parties in Scotland and others whose task was to report on the operational needs and working methods of the Scottish Parliament and develop proposals for rules of procedure and Standing Orders which the Parliament might adopt.

Convener: the person who chairs a committee. It can apply to a man or a woman and is therefore a better term than chairman.

Court of Session: the highest court of civil jurisdiction in Scotland. Under certain conditions, appeal may be made from it to the House of Lords.

Declarator: an order of a Scottish court which declares the rights of a party.

EC: the European Community which the UK joined in 1973. The term EC law is the correct term for matters of law relating to the European Community Treaty.

EU: the European Union. Strictly speaking, this is different from the European Community and reflects a movement towards closer political and monetary union by the members of the European Community. The term EU is correctly applied to EU countries or EU citizens.

ECHR: the European Convention on Human Rights (now incorporated in the Human Rights Act 1998).

Executive Bill: a Bill proposed by the party or parties which form the Scottish Executive.

First Minister: The person who is the head of the Scottish Executive, normally the Leader of the political party with the largest number of seats.

High Court of Justiciary: the highest court of criminal jurisdiction in Scotland. There is no appeal from this court to the House of Lords.

Interdict: an order of a Scottish court which prohibits conduct.

Intra vires: within the powers of the Scottish Parliament as laid down in the Scotland Act.

Judicial Committee of the Privy Council (JCPC): a committee which consists of the Lord Chancellor, Lords of Appeal in Ordinary (the Law Lords) and all Privy Councillors who hold, or have held, high judicial office, together with certain distinguished Commonwealth judges. For the purposes of legal proceedings relating to devolution issues, the Commonwealth judges are excluded. In practice, the composition of the Judicial Committee of the Privy Council is very similar to the House of Lords when it sits as a court of appeal.

Junior Scottish Ministers: Members of the Scottish Parliament who are appointed to assist the Scottish Ministers.

Law Officers: in Scotland these are the Lord Advocate and the Solicitor General. The Lord Advocate is the principal legal adviser to the Scottish Government and is also the head of the system of public prosecution of crime and the investigation of deaths in Scotland. The Solicitor General is the deputy to the Lord Advocate. They are members of the Scottish Executive, but they need not be elected as MSPs.

Legislative competence: areas within which the Scottish Parliament can make laws as laid down in the Scotland Act 1998.

MSP: a Member of the Scottish Parliament.

Order in Council: a form of secondary legislation, made in a more formal manner than a Statutory Instrument.

Parliamentary Bureau: the PB consists of the Presiding Officer and a representative of each political party represented by five or more MSPs. There are also provisions for representation by parties with fewer than five MSPs. Its main functions are the organisation of the business programme of the Parliament and the establishment, remit and membership of the Parliament's committees and sub-committees.

Presiding Officer: the MSP who chairs the meetings of the full Parliament and is responsible for keeping order during proceedings in Parliament. The role is very similar to that of the Speaker of the House of Commons.

Private Bills/Private Legislation: legislation promoted through the

Parliament, usually by bodies such as local authorities, occasionally by private individuals.

Quorum: the minimum number of members who must be present for business to be undertaken.

Regional members: members of the Scottish Parliament who are returned from the regional lists drawn up by the political parties or as individual candidates on the regional lists as a result of the second votes cast in the election. In the first Scottish Parliament, there are 56 regional members.

Schedule: part of an Act of Parliament which may be found at the end of the sections of an Act. It contains matters of details which cannot conveniently be included in the body of the Act such as the list of reserved matters in the Scotland Act. Not every Act has a Schedule. The Scotland Act 1998 contains nine Schedules.

Scottish Administration: this term covers the First Minister and the other members of the Scottish Executive, junior Scottish Ministers, certain offices such as the Registrar General, and their staff.

Scottish Constitutional Convention (SCC): a group consisting of members representing various political parties in Scotland (excluding the Conservatives and the Scottish National Party) and members from a wide range of Scottish civic society, such as the trade unions and the churches. The group produced various documents in which were laid out proposals for a Scottish Parliament. Much of the Scotland Act is influenced by their work.

Scottish Executive: the members of the Scottish Government, *i.e.* the First Minister, the Scottish Ministers, and the Law Officers.

Scottish Parliamentary Corporate Body (SPCB): the body which will provide the Scottish Parliament with staff, services and property.

Secondary legislation: legislation normally made by Ministers which implements policy already agreed by an Act of Parliament or an Act of the Scottish Parliament. It is also known as **subordinate** or **delegated legislation**. The most common forms are **statutory instruments** and **Orders in Council**.

Standing Orders: the rules which govern the proceedings in the Parliament.

Statutory Instruments: one of the most common forms of secondary legislation.

Sub judice: currently subject to legal proceedings.

Subordinate legislation: see **secondary legislation**.

Ultra vires: outside the powers of the Scottish Parliament as defined in the Scotland Act 1998.

FURTHER READING

This section gives information about a number of publications which provide more detail of the issues dealt with in this book. It will be obvious that the list does not attempt to be comprehensive, but rather seeks to give some suggestions as to where readers interested in the subject matter of this book can turn for further reading. Most of the publications given below themselves contain references to further material on the subject.

Alice Brown, David McCrone, and Lindsay Paterson, *Politics and Society in Scotland* (2nd edn, 1998: Macmillan, Basingstoke). This book provides a comprehensive survey of politics and society in Scotland in the latter part of the twentieth century, in a longer historical context. It pays particular attention to the pressure for constitutional change up to and beyond the 1997 General Election. The book features an extremely comprehensive guide to further reading.

Bernard Crick and David Millar, *To Make the Parliament of Scotland a Model for Democracy* (2nd edn, 1997: John Wheatley Centre, Edinburgh). The authors proposed draft Standing Orders for the Scottish Parliament, and many of their proposals were reflected in the final CSG Report. The authors also looked at the relationships after devolution between Scotland and Westminster, and between Scotland and Europe.

The Constitution Unit, *Scotland's Parliament: Fundamentals for a New Scotland Act* (1996). This report examined the practicalities of the scheme for devolution proposed by the Scottish Constitutional Convention, and its work was influential in determining many of the details of the devolution scheme eventually adopted by the Government.

Report of the Consultative Steering Group on the Scottish Parliament, *Shaping Scotland's Parliament* (1998: Stationery Office, Edinburgh). The Scottish Parliament's Standing Orders are largely based on the recommendations contained in this report. It also contains useful appendices, dealing amongst other matters with equal opportunities issues, financial issues, and information and communications technologies. The report also lists (at page 91) various items of research commissioned and published by the CSG, examining in more detail some aspects of the operation of the new Parliament. The report is still a useful source of information, even though some of its contents have, of course, been superseded now that Parliament is up-and-running.

Michael Fry, *Patronage and Principle: A Political History of Modern Scotland* (1987: Aberdeen University Press, Aberdeen). A provocative, but thorough and valuable, history of Scottish politics from the 1830s to the 1980s.

Himsworth and Munro, *The Scotland Act 1998* (W. Green, 1999) This book contains the full text of the Scotland Act, together with extensive annotation and explanations of its provisions. It is a particularly useful volume for both students and practitioners.

James Kellas, *The Scottish Political System* (4th edn, 1989: Cambridge University Press, Cambridge). Widely regarded as the standard textbook on Scottish government and politics. It provides a general historical and institutional analysis of Scottish politics, although obviously it does not cover more recent developments.

Page, Reid and Ross, *A Guide to the Scotland Act 1998* (Butterworths, 1999).

Scotland in the Union: A Partnership for Good (HMSO, Cm 2225).

Scottish Constitutional Convention, *Scotland's Parliament. Scotland's Right* (1995: Edinburgh). The final report of the Constitutional Convention containing its proposals for a Scottish Parliament, upon which the Government's proposals in *Scotland's Parliament* drew considerably.

Scottish Office, *Scotland's Parliament* (1997, White Paper, Cm. 3658: Stationery Office). This is the White Paper that gave the details of the new Labour Government's proposals for Scottish devolution, which were placed before the electorate in the referendum of 11th September 1997.

Scottish Affairs. This journal is published by the Unit for the Study of Government at the University of Edinburgh. Since 1992 (and from 1977 in its predecessor *The Scottish Government Year Book*) it has regularly featured articles on all aspects of Scottish devolution, and Scottish politics in general. It also carries regular book reviews and lists of books received.

The Scottish Parliament itself has an excellent website (www.scottish parliament.uk) which provides up-to-date details of its legislative programme and the work of its committees, as well as general information about the Parliament and its members. Full details of the business discussed in the Parliament can be found in the pages of its website containing its *Minutes of Proceedings* and the Scottish Parliament Official Report. The Parliament's website provides a range of links to other websites concerned with aspects of Scottish government and public life, and to the websites of other Parliaments and Assemblies. The Parliament also produces *What's Happening in the Scottish Parliament* (published by The Stationery Office, for the Scottish Parliamentary Corporate Body, and familiarly known as WHISP), providing a regular report of its business and activities.

The Stationery Office, Guidance on Public Bills; produced by the Clerking Services Directorate of the Scottish Parliament, mainly for use by MSPs.

Two new journals, *Scottish Constitutional and Administrative Law & Practice* (published by CLT Professional Publishing Ltd) and *Scottish Parliament Law Review* (published by W. Green) have been launched since the establishment of the Scottish Parliament. Both contain a range of articles and briefing material about legal issues arising from the new devolved constitutional arrangements.

INDEX